Wisdom from the Edge

EXPERTISE

CULTURES AND
TECHNOLOGIES
OF KNOWLEDGE

EDITED BY DOMINIC BOYER

A list of titles in this series is available at cornellpress.cornell.edu.

Wisdom from the Edge

Writing Ethnography in Turbulent Times

Paul Stoller

Cornell University Press

Ithaca and London

First published 2023 by Cornell University Press

Library of Congress Cataloging-in-Publication Data

Names: Stoller, Paul, author.
Title: Wisdom from the edge : writing ethnography in turbulent times / Paul Stoller.
Description: Ithaca : Cornell University Press, 2023. | Series: Expertise series | Includes bibliographical references and index.
Identifiers: LCCN 2023003109 (print) | LCCN 2023003110 (ebook) | ISBN 9781501770654 (hardcover) | ISBN 9781501770661 (paperback) | ISBN 9781501770883 (pdf) | ISBN 9781501770678 (epub)
Subjects: LCSH: Ethnology—Authorship. | Ethnology—Moral and ethical aspects. | Ethnology—Philosophy. | Ethnologists—Attitudes.
Classification: LCC GN345 .S854 2023 (print) | LCC GN345 (ebook) | DDC 305.8—dc23/eng/20230210
LC record available at https://lccn.loc.gov/2023003109
LC ebook record available at https://lccn.loc.gov/2023003110

For Adamu Jenitongo, Kada Mounmouni, Amadu Zima, Abdoulaye Cisse, and Fatouma Seyni, the West African elders who taught me so well

Contents

Prelude

Early one morning during ethnographic fieldwork in Tillabéri, Niger, the hottest town in the hottest country in the world, I sat on a beautifully woven palm frond mat in the shade of Adamu Jenitongo's thatch spirit hut. For several months I had been living in my mentor's compound, which he had built at the edge of the village. At sunrise Adamu Jenitongo, my teacher and an important Songhay healer, had told me that he wanted to talk to me about important matters.

Shortly thereafter, he arrived with a brazier full of hot embers. His grandson followed behind bringing a porcelain platter on which he had placed a teapot, one large water glass, and two shot glasses.

Adamu Jenitongo poured water into the teapot, measured a shot glass full of strong Chinese green tea, and put it on the embers. "We'll drink tea and talk about life."

Not knowing how to respond, I sat quietly.

When the tea water boiled my teacher added sugar and went through the pouring ritual, emptying the steeping tea into the water glass and returning it to the teapot—three times. Finally, he poured tea into our shot glasses, and we began to sip.

As we sipped the strong tea, we looked at one another for a long moment.

"You have been coming here for years," he said, breaking the silence.

I nodded.

"And you've learned a great deal."

"I have much more to learn," I admitted.

"You do," he said. "But today I want you to open your ears and understand what's important."

"I am listening, Baba."

He turned his head toward the east and looked beyond the edge of the village to take in the bush—wild, uninhabited space where powerful spirits live. "Good," he said, still looking at the bush. "Times are bad. People have lost respect for the old words and for the old ways." He turned and looked at me. "Our fathers and mothers understood how bad it is for people to speak with two mouths and feel with two hearts. People who speak with two mouths and feel with two hearts anger the spirits of the bush. When the bush is angry there is not enough rain. When the bush is angry there is too much rain. When the bush is angry locusts eat our crops and sickness kills our people." He sipped more tea.

Several cranes flew overhead. A donkey brayed in the distance.

Shaking his head, my mentor continued. "Every day our people do things to anger the bush. Every day I make offerings to the bush to set things right, to bring a one-mouth, one-heart balance to the world. That is what the elders taught me. That is my work." He finished his tea. "That's what I want to teach you. I hope that my work can become your work."

The bush is angry today. After the temperature in Portland, Oregon, soared to more than 112 degrees in June 2021, is it not perhaps time to rethink our two-mouths/two-hearts priorities? After wildfires and floods have brought on mass destruction and the loss of life in Europe and North America, is it not perhaps time to critically assess our two-mouths/two-hearts behavioral practices? After COVID-19's latest wave has brought more disease, death, and economic despair, is it not perhaps time to reform the environmentally destructive extractive practices that anger the bush? Is it not time to acknowledge the wisdom of people like Adamu Jenitongo and admit that human beings who live in the village have never been the masters of the bush?

Wisdom from the Edge is my attempt to transform Adamu Jenitongo's work into my work. In this book I hope to demonstrate what anthropologists might do to contribute to the social and cultural changes that can shape a social future of well-being and viability. In the following pages, I attempt to show how anthropologists can use sensuously described ethnographic narratives to powerfully communicate their slowly developed insights to a wide range of audiences. These insights are filled with wisdom about how respect for nature—the bush—is central to the future of *Homo sapiens*.

When I began to write anthropology, my intent, like that of most of the colleagues in my cohort, was to produce work that might refine theory, which meant that I tried to adhere to most of the expository traditions that scholarly publications and publishers required: well-sourced, logically contoured arguments that might increase comprehension of the particularities of kinship, language use, economic exchange, social transformations, and/or magic and sorcery. Such writing, I thought, might increase our understanding of the whys and wherefores of what Hannah Arendt long ago called "the human condition." Although I found such pursuit intellectually satisfying, I wondered if the theoretical insights about which I had written would make sense to non-anthropologists. I also wondered what my Songhay teachers, who conveyed their wisdom to me and others through stories, would think of the discourse they would find in academic texts. These realizations compelled me to try to write anthropological works that would appeal to a broad range of readers.

Following the advice of Songhay elders like Adamu Jenitongo, I began to develop texts that foregrounded narratives evoking anthropological insights, a move that could possibly make my anthropological work more publicly accessible. At first this strategy seemed to work to some degree. Even so, I still felt that my work only attracted a limited audience of readers. Thinking about the much-admired work of anthropologists working actively on issues of climate change, inequality, and racism, I wondered what I might do to contribute. And so, I began to write blogs on public platforms like *Huffington Post* and *Psychology Today*. Regular blogging about the anthropological aspects of politics, the nature of social science, West African social life, and health and well-being not only contributed to the spread of anthropological insights but also sharpened my prose. That development, in turn, encouraged me to design and teach ethnographic writing courses for scholars—in all stages of their careers. In those courses scholars have worked on essays and blogs that foreground narratives highlighting the sensuousness of space and place, the idiosyncrasies of dialogue, and the particularities of character, all to bring into sensuous relief the drama of social life, all to make anthropological insights more accessible to the public.

This book emerges from three sources: (1) the ethnographic writing courses I have offered for more than ten years; (2) the impact of sensuous description in the artful composition of ethnographic prose and film; and not least (3) the depth and breadth of the wisdom of indigenous peoples like the Songhay people of Niger and Mali in West Africa, where I for many years had the privilege to live and learn. The importance of space/place, dialogue, and character, of course, is central to conveying important anthropological insights to the public. The key to artful representation in prose and film devolves from the evocation of the senses. Sensuous description, in turn, is central to the ethnographic presentation of indigenous wisdom. In our troubled times my hope is that *Wisdom from the Edge* will show present and future ethnographers one way to present this much-needed knowledge to the public.

Acknowledgments

M any people and institutions have been involved in the process of transforming an idea into this book, which means that I am profoundly grateful to the institutions that have funded my ongoing research and to trusted colleagues, friends, and family who have graciously given me much-needed critique and guidance. *Wisdom from the Edge* is the result of long-term field research in the Republic of Niger and New York City. For funds that enabled my ethnographic research I thank the US Department of Education (Fulbright Research Program), the American Philosophical Society, the NATO Postdoctoral Fellowship in Science Program, the Wenner-Gren Foundation for Anthropological Research, the National Science Foundation, and West Chester University (the Faculty Development and College of Arts and Sciences research programs). The John Simon Guggenheim Foundation, the School for Advanced Research in Santa Fe, New Mexico, the National Endowment for the Humanities, and West Chester University (sabbatical program) provided funds that gave me time for writing. My writing workshops and courses have been sponsored by the University of Manchester, the University of Bern, the Free University of Berlin, the University of Helsinki, Queen's University,

Belfast, the University of Amsterdam, the Institute of Graduate Studies, University of Geneva, the University of Ghana, Legon, and the Northwest Creative Writing Institute at Lewis and Clark College.

For past and ongoing conversations about anthropology and ethnographic writing I thank Ana Mariella Bacigalupo, Anna Badkhen, Ruth Behar, Dominic Boyer, Anne Cassiman, Evi Chatzipangiotidou, Rupert Cox, Sienna Craig, Filip De Boeck, Valerian DeSousa, Michael Di Giovine, Jean-Paul Dumont, James Fernandez, Juan Antonio Flores Martos, Steven Friedson, Marina Gold, Alma Gottlieb, Philip Graham, Sarah Green, Sten Hagberg, Ulf Hannerz, Mark Harris, Paul Henley, Lisbet Holtedahl, Andrew Irving, Michael D. Jackson, Bruce Kapferer, Shahram Khosravi, Sergio Lopez, Christos Lynteris, Jonathan Marion, Marie Mauze, Fiona McDonald, Carole McGranahan, Cristina Moreno, Joanne Mulcahy, Fiona Murphy, A. David Napier, the late Pauline Napier, Kirin Narayan, Priya Nelson, David Nugent, Devaka Premawardhana, Nigel Rapport, the late Jay Ruby, Michaela Schaeuble, Don Seeman, Tony Simpson, Johannes Sjoberg, Patricia Smith, Yana Stainova, Katie Stewart, Barbara Tedlock, the late Dennis Tedlock, the late Edith Turner, Rory Turner, Gina Ulysse, Anna-Maria Volkmann, and Helena Wulff. For their ongoing support and inspiration, I thank members of my family and my close circle of friends, Mitchell and Sheri Stoller, Lauren Stoller, Betsy and Oren Davidian, Beverly Gendelman, Robert Rosenberg and Lisa Ruggeri, Ken and Carole Derow, Melina McConatha, Lauren McConatha, Korey Jones, Helena McConatha Rosle, Roxanne Spellman, Vera Spellman, Afsaneh Tahmaseb Regimand, Soraya Tahmaseb Shultz, Sirus Tahmaseb, Afsheen Tahmaseb, Mozi Tahmaseb, John and Donna Chernoff, T. David Brent, Fabio Fernandez, the late Frauke Schnell, Emilia Schnell Fernandez, and Luisa Schnell Fernandez. I owe a debt of gratitude to all the scholars who have participated in my ethnographic writing courses. I look forward to reading their future works. Finally, Jasmin Tahmaseb McConatha has made me a better scholar, writer, and person. Her incisive comments on *Wisdom from the Edge* have substantially improved the quality of the text.

Earlier versions of some of the material in the book have appeared in *Revista de Antropologia Iberoamerican* 16: 17–37 and *Anthropological Quarterly* 91(1): 393–401; *Swedish Journal of Anthropology* 3(1): 11–21; *Anthropology and Humanism* 46(1): 69–80; *Amuse-Bouche: The Taste of Art* (Museum Tinguely, 2020), 98–104; *Peripheral Methodologies: Unlearning, Not-knowing and Ethnographic Limits* (Martínez, Di Puppo, and Frederiksen, eds., 2021), ix–xiv; and *The Routledge International Handbook of Ethnographic Film and Video* (Phillip Vannini, ed., 2020), 348–55.

Introduction

WRITING ETHNOGRAPHY IN
TURBULENT TIMES

Nature is on the inside

Cézanne

In May 2020 gunmen riding on motorcycles looted shops, stole cattle, and killed twenty people in the Tillabéri Region of Niger—the latest incident in a two-year cycle of Al Qaeda–inspired violence. This news filled me with sadness. Having spent many years in Tillabéri I harbor wonderful memories of my Tillabéri friends, of sweeping vistas of the Niger River snaking its way through majestic dunes and sandstone buttes, and of the hunger-inducing aromas of kebabs cooking on makeshift grills. My mentor, Adamu Jenitongo, lived at the edge of Tillabéri in a dune-top compound, the site of many compellingly beautiful traditional religious rituals. The widespread tolerance that had once characterized this community had been replaced with religious zealotry.

The dysfunction that has shredded the social fabric in Tillabéri, Niger, is, of course, not an isolated phenomenon. These days we live in a world in which we can no longer ignore systemic racism, ethnic discrimination, religious intolerance, and income inequality, not to forget the social and economic devastation of the coronavirus pandemic.

How can anthropologists meet the challenges of our turbulent times?

In this chapter I suggest that we confront our obligations as scholars and admit that many of our long-standing methods and denotative conventions of representation are no longer in sync with the state of contemporary social, political, environmental, and economic dysfunction. In the coming months there are important questions that I ask myself:

—How can we adjust to the emotional, social, and economic dislocations caused by the COVID-19 pandemic?
—How can we prepare for and adjust to future pandemics?
—How can we plan for the social upheavals that climate change will produce?

In anthropology we spend a great deal of time thinking, reading, and writing about these existential issues. At times our reliance on established conventions of representation has limited our ability to extend our insights to the public. To meet the existential challenges of difficult times, I propose that anthropologists plunge into the art of ethnography, in which ethnographers sensuously articulate dimensions of locality, language, and character. Borrowing techniques from film, poetry, and fiction, I intend to show how artfully inspired ethnographers can craft ethnographic narratives in text and film that can connect the public to the idiosyncrasies of people and place. In so doing, I argue, an artful ethnography has the potential to bring to the public sphere the nuanced indigenous wisdom of others, the very foundation of anthropological insight. Such wisdom that sits at the edge of the village can set a course that ultimately leads to meaningful change, social justice, and the future viability of our species.

For me, artful ethnographic practice begins with Maurice Merleau-Ponty's brief text, *Eye and Mind*, which is undisputedly one of the most influential philosophical essays of the twentieth century.[1] In it, the great phenomenologist suggests that the work of art is a pathway to an embodied enlightenment that can enable us to practice what Michael Jackson has called "the art of life."[2] The key premise of *Eye and Mind* is that nature, as the artist Paul Cézanne suggested, is on the inside. To know nature, then, is to know the texture of inner space. As Merleau-Ponty wrote, the "quality, light, color, and depth which are there before us are there only because they awaken an echo in our body and because the body welcomes them."[3] Such an orientation is a critique of scientific positivism. For Merleau-Ponty and Cézanne there is an inner reality of things that supplements the "objective" reality that scholars have extracted from their observations of the world. To operationalize this inner reality into hypotheses, formulae, and laws condemns us to a superficial apprehension of the physical and social worlds. Merleau-Ponty believed that the painter is our guide on the path to what he called the *there-is*. The painter savors the life that resides in the inner dimensions of things. Indeed, the painter, like other artists, feels the reverberations that can create awareness in the eye and mind of the person who confronts the sensory splendor of the world.

Merleau-Ponty's writing about art is not some vague mystical journey into the unseen or the sensory unconscious. In *Eye and Mind*, he suggests that artists are our guides to the *there-is* because they open their being to the world. "Indeed, we cannot imagine how a mind could paint. It is by lending his body to the world that the artist changes the world into paintings."[4] Put another way, the act of painting is a metaphor for sensing the world from the inside. In *Le monologue du peintre*, Georges Charbonnier wrote of a conversation he had with the painter André Marchand during which the latter underscored sentiments that Paul Klee often expressed in his lectures. Charbonnier wrote: "In a forest I have felt many times over that it was not I who looked at the forest. Some days I felt that the trees were looking at me. I was there, listening. . . . I think that the painter must be penetrated by the universe and not penetrate it. . . . I expect to be inwardly submerged, buried. I paint to break out."[5]

Are artists alone in their inner sensibilities? Merleau-Ponty charts a course toward a sensuous turn in our observations and our representations of those observations. Such a turn, of course, can be applied to anthropologists and their representations. How do we make the indeterminacies of existence intelligible? How can we bring them to life? Consider Nietzsche's thoughts on scientific intelligibility. He wrote that the mission of science

> is to make existence intelligible and thereby justified. . . . Socrates and his successors, down to our day, have considered all moral and sentimental accomplishments—noble deeds, compassion, self-sacrifice, heroism . . . to be ultimately derived from the dialectic of knowledge and therefore teachable. . . . But science, spurred on by its energetic notions, approaches irresistibly those outer limits where the optimism of logic must collapse. . . . When the inquirer, having pushed to the circumference, realizes how logic in that place curls about itself and bites its own tail, he is struck with a new kind of perception, a tragic perception, which requires, to make it tolerable, the remedy of art.[6]

By way of Nietzsche, Cézanne, and Klee, Merleau-Ponty suggested that scholarly discourse is limited. Denotation or telling has a limited capacity to describe the inner dimensions of nature or the deep recesses of the human existence. The deep exploration of the human condition requires, for Merleau-Ponty, the remedy of art (evocation or showing). Indeed, Merleau-Ponty has much to say about the power of evocation in art and in artful prose. "The words, the lines and the colors which express me," he wrote, "come from me as my gestures are torn from me by what I want to say, the way my gestures are and by what I want to do. . . . In the art of prose, words carry the speaker and listener into a common universe by drawing both toward a new signification through their power to designate in excess of their accepted definition."[7]

Merleau-Ponty goes on to suggest that the "words most charged with philosophy are not necessarily those that contain what they say, but rather those that most energetically open upon being, because they more closely convey the life of the whole and make our habitual evidences vibrate until they disjoin."[8] In this way, writers—or painters, for that matter—use what Merleau-Ponty calls "the indirect voice" to evoke the "brute and wild being" of the world.

As my summary of the political, social, and cultural instability in Tillabéri suggests, we live in complex and unstable times. There are no clear answers to the political, social, and intellectual problems of our era. Given the multiplex dimensions of contemporary life, is it still possible to make sense of the human condition? Can we apprehend Merleau-Ponty's brute and wild being? And if we can experience such a revelatory and brute consciousness, will it deepen our sensibilities, our capacity to understand the imponderables of living in the world? Do artists and anthropologists have a role to play in this important contemporary endeavor? What can Merleau-Ponty's *Eye and Mind* teach us about confronting the darkness that has swept over contemporary social life?[9] Can we squeeze small measures of well-being from the speedy chaos of social life? Can anthropological insight chart a path that leads to a life well lived? In two of Michael Jackson's latest books—one on reinventing philosophical anthropology and one on the power of art in shaping the contours of social life—the anthropologist-poet explores these vexing questions with powerful perspicacity.

In *As Wide as the World Is Wise*, Jackson elegantly explores the spaces between things—murky spaces in which human beings are always already, to borrow from Jacques Derrida, situated.[10] These are spaces that escape brute categorization. They are spaces that are defiantly non-concrete—spaces that require the evocation of art and artful scholarship. For his epigraph, Jackson quotes Derrida, who wrote that "the logocentrism of Greek metaphysics will always be haunted . . . by the 'absolutely other' to the extent that the Logos can never englobe everything. There is always something which escapes, something different, something other and opaque which refuses to be totalized into a homogeneous identity."[11]

In this wonderfully crafted work, Jackson is our guide to those existential spaces in which, according to Nietzsche, "logic curls about itself and bites its own tail." These are spaces that are different and opaque. After more than forty years of fieldwork in West Africa and Australia, after a lifetime of reading, reflection, and writing about living-in-the-world, Jackson describes how his experience directed him to follow the sinuous, non-totalizing path between things—between the one and the many, between identity and difference, between ourselves and others, between the personal and the professional, between belief and experience, between being and thought, between fate and free will, between center and periphery. *As Wide as the World Is Wise*, then, is a book that artfully explores the imaginative spaces between anthropology and philosophy. Indeed, in this rich, deep, and textured book Jackson's erudition demonstrates with eloquence how the messy specificity that characterizes ethnography enriches our thought. Consider this thought-provoking passage: "Are philosophy and anthropology not also ways of creating appearances—whether of order and understanding—that provide us with a sense of purchase on the elusive face of human existence? And are not philosophers and anthropologists the cousins-german of the trickster heroes who figure in all traditions?"[12]

Indeed, Jackson provides a plethora of ethnographic and experiential examples that demonstrate how our anthropological and philosophical cogitations "never englobe everything," to return yet again to Derrida: "There is always something that escapes."[13] Things are always impermanent. Our experience, feelings, thoughts are continuously evolving. Our lived reality is one that confounds everyday certainty. We are all between things. Jackson writes that in life we find ourselves in "a perpetual oscillation between engaging with the world and seeking distance, respite, or release from it. No matter what vernacular idiom is employed to capture this oscillation—philosopher's hut, the open field, the contrast between town and bush, theological images of earth and ether, existential tensions between home and the world—the dilemma persists of how to balance and reconcile these competing imperatives or discover how one can live with their incommensurability."[14]

How can we live in the intellectual and experiential turbulence of spaces between things? How can we bear the intellectual and existential fruits of cultivating what John Keats called "negative capability," the capacity to live with incommensurability, the inchoateness of which stretches the imagination and sparks creativity?[15]

Jackson considers these questions in another recent work, *The Work of Art*, in which he rethinks Durkheim's *The Elementary Forms of Religious Life* from a decidedly phenomenological perspective.[16] Drawing inspiration from the aforementioned *Eye and Mind* (1964), Jackson tacks between personal reflection and an interpretation of a varied group of artists, including the mesmerizing productions of Australian Aboriginals. By way of his analysis and his personal reflections, Jackson demonstrates how art is not an inert element of representation but a dynamic force that can transform life. The work of art, then, can enable us to open our being to the world, prompting writers and painters to see—to think from the inside.

In the end, Jackson extends his analysis of artistic works to write about the art of life, which, Jackson states,

> is thus an art of making the world appear perennially new by what Rimbaud called "*un long, immense et raisonne dérèglement de tous sens*"—an endless play of light and dark, bitter and sweet, sound and silence, hard and soft, acrid and fragrant. Against the grain of inscribed habits of thought, action, and perception, art—whether graphic, sculptural, musical, verbal, gestural or kinesic—involves a honing, a practicing, a play of our sensibilities, which bring us to a place that seems to surpass the familiar, the known, the expected, surprising us, taking our breath away, opening our eyes, transforming our understanding, and, ultimately, re-creating ourselves.[17]

Between the lines of this book Jackson demonstrates that art can transport us to the creative and imaginative spaces between things. He shows us how art can reshape our being in the world, transforming our inner turmoil into the outward beauty of prose, poetry, drama, sculpture, and painting—works that move us.

Can anthropologists, most of whom have conducted extensive ethnographic research, follow obscure tracks that crisscross the deserts of academic discourse and find illumination? Following the embodied insights of Merleau-Ponty's *Eye and Mind* and the wisdom found in Michael Jackson's *The Work of Art*, can we embrace the art of ethnography? In the end, can we learn how to convey to the public our important and slowly developed insights about the human condition?

Many scholars reduce ethnography to a set of practices. Ethnographers, after all, conduct fieldwork in a variety of settings. Fieldwork consists of Malinowski's celebrated, if not conceptually flawed, notion of participant observation—being there. Trying to observe while you participate is no easy feat. Even so, thousands of ethnographers have attempted this oxymoronic method as they struggle to conduct a census, engage in informal and semiformal interviews, or attend a ritual that they may photograph or film. In the same vein, ethnographers are supposed to record their participant-observations in field notes, some purely observational, some more personal. These field notes combined with field photographs and field films become the foundation for constructing a representation. In the end these ethnographic texts or films contribute to the ethnographic record. Is this not the set of procedures that we teach future anthropologists?

Beyond the rigorous set of rules that define ethnographic research, the potential distinctiveness of ethnographic texts often gets lost in the fog or institutional expectation. The expected anthropological monograph should have an introduction, a review of the relevant literature, presentation of data, a discussion of the data, and a conclusion in which the work's disciplinary significance, stated by the author in the introduction, is reaffirmed. These academic conventions of representation often lead to the production of turgid texts of limited appeal. Given the economic privations of contemporary publishing, editors now have a less than enthusiastic interest in publishing anthropological works.

One way to change this representational dilemma is to engage in the art of ethnography, in which writers sensuously articulate dimensions of locality, language, and character. Borrowing the insights of Merleau-Ponty and following the expository example of inspirational writers like Toni Morrison, James Agee, Annie Dillard, Michael Chabon, and Walter Mosley, artfully inspired ethnographers can craft ethnographic descriptions such that readers come to know the dynamic idiosyncrasies of people and place. In so doing an artful ethnography has the potential to spread far and wide our slowly developed anthropological insights.

An artful ethnography can bring to life ethnographic spaces and places. It can give readers a sense of locality—one of the great gifts that ethnography brings to the world. How can writers use words to sensuously describe a landscape, a wall, a road, a house, or a room? For me, writers should try to describe a space or place as if it were alive—with feelings and memories. In so doing, writers should attempt to let the sights, smells, sounds, and texture of a space/place dictate how to describe it. This technique borrows from Paul Klee's technique of opening his being to the forest and painting it to "break out." In this painterly style of describing ethnographic spaces, it is important to highlight salient features. It is also important to imagine what a particular room, house, tree, or pathway has witnessed. When I recently observed a majestic baobab tree, which grows next to the Institute of African Studies at the University of Ghana, Legon, I wondered what history that tree had witnessed.

Sensuously setting an ethnographic scene can captivate readers, compelling them to turn the page. Here are some examples in which writers evoke space and place. Consider how James Agee, author of *Let Us Now Praise Famous Men*, uses a brief description of a sharecropper's house to create a sensuously palpable description of life in rural Alabama during the American Depression:

> Every few minutes George would get up and open the door a foot or so, and it showed always the same picture; that end of the hallway mud and under water, where the planks lay flush to the ground; the opposite wall; the open kitchen; blown leaves beyond the kitchen window; a segment of the clay rear yard where rain beat on rain beat on rain beat on rain as would beat out the brains of the earth and stood in a bristling smoky grass of water a foot high.[18]

FIGURE 1
The baobab tree at the Institute of African Studies, University of Ghana, Legon.
© Paul Stoller.

Here is a snippet from Kirin Narayan's wonderful book, *Storytell-ers, Saints, and Scoundrels*. Notice how Narayan uses this short de-scriptive passage to introduce her book's main character and set the storytelling tone for the text that follows.

> Swamiji lay in his deck chair. His legs, bare below the knee, were out-stretched, but his eyes were alert. He was chatting with the assem-bled company about other Gurus. He had told us anecdotes about an eccentric saint, then about a child who was proclaimed to be the reincarnation of a popular Guru by some people but dismissed by others as a fraud. Like any day when Swamiji's doors were open, a motley array of visitors was present: Indians from various regions and castes, and a handful of Westerners. I sat among these visi-tors, cross-legged against the wall on the women's side of the room. A breeze lifted the curtains behind the deck chair and, suspended in the moment, I set my notebook and tape recorder aside to relax into the flow of Swamiji's colloquial Hindi. Yet I was soon shaken out of my lulled state, for Swamiji, leaping to another topic with his usual dexterity, now announced that there was a difference between the educated and uneducated. At this point his eyes, blurred and magnified by heavy glasses, became fixated on me.[19]

A more contemporary example of sensuous ethnographic scene setting comes from Anna Badkhen and her 2018 work of creative nonfiction, *Fisherman's Blues: A West African Community at Sea*. Follow how Badkhen describes a dawn at sea near Joal, Senegal's largest artisanal fishing port.

> Dawn spills astern: lavender, violet, golden. Capillary waves gen-tly scale the ocean all the way to the horizon. Wind clots low fog. The *Sakhari Souare* glides at full throttle west-southwest, rolls over lazy six-foot swells. The shore's low skyline of baobab, eucalyptus and doum palm flashes in the light, sinks into the sea. Its bruised cumulus vanishes, too. Black against the banded east, a seabird,

an early riser, falls out of the fog and scoops something out of the water and banks away. The pirogue's six crew balance spreadeagled on the thwarts and on the foredeck, dig their bare soles into the slippery wood, lean into one another, watch the sea for fish.[20]

In his luminous novel, *Small Country*, Gaël Faye, an emerging novelist, writes lyrically about the murderous times of his childhood in Burundi. In this short passage he demonstrates how to describe a scene that captures the ethos of place.

Nothing is sweeter than the moment when the sun sinks behind the ridge of mountains. Dusk brings with it the cool of evening and warm colors that deepen with every minute. This is the hour that marks a change in rhythm. People head home from work at a leisurely pace, the night watchmen come on duty, and neighbors sit out in front of their gates. There is silence before the toads and crickets start up. Often it is the perfect time for a game of football, or for sitting with a friend on the low wall above the gutter, for gluing your ear to the radio, or for visiting a neighbor.[21]

A final example of the sensuous evocation of space comes from Lucas Bessire's gripping memoir/ethnography, *Running Out: In Search of Water on the High Plains*. It is a story that cries out for the sensuous evocation of space. Here Bessire writes of his reconnection to the land of his childhood—an array of fields in dire need of fast disappearing water.

After fifteen years, the land matched my memories of it. I recalled precisely the vault of space, the circled sky the most dominant feature and the sun a physical weight. Grids of stubble that rotate every half-mile, from corn to wheat to sorghum to corn. Each field a parable about boys who became men by learning to plow every inch, by knowing what not to know, by never learning or by never coming back.

The road dead-ends at the break of the now dry Cimarron River, where the tablelands fall abruptly to a ribbon of short-grass nestled in a river bend with sage and sand hills rising to the south. Here stands the Little Rock House. Named after century-old concrete walls and corrals, it was once my great-grandfather's cattle camp. It is where I spent most of my adolescent summers and it is where my father returned to live out his years amid broken flints and buried bison bones.[22]

As these examples demonstrate, the sensuous description of place and space is a key ingredient in the recipe for an artful ethnography that evokes the *there-is*.

There is, of course, more to artful ethnography than setting a scene. In any kind of artful writing, what can be more difficult than crafting dialogue? The distinctive way that a person speaks is a window into her or his character, motivations, and emotional states. Important as it is, artful dialogue is often absent in ethnographic texts. Informant talk is often relegated to the indented block texts of transcribed interviews, which usually give no indication of the idiosyncrasies of said informant's talk. In addition, informant talk is often transformed into indirect speech, in which the informant's speech is summarized in the ethnographer's explicative prose.[23] In artful ethnography, scholars borrow dialogue techniques from fiction and creative nonfiction writers who use them to convey important information and build character.

But is it possible to write dialogue that perfectly captures every aspect of a person's speech? I have found that crafting dialogue is the most challenging aspect of writing both fiction and ethnography. In my experience West Africans tend to speak to one another with a complex formality. Depending on the time of day, there are multiple formal greetings. What's more, people often refer to one another indirectly—even in the context of the speech situation.

Rather than calling one another by name, West African interlocuters often refrain from mentioning names. Instead, they might refer to a person as "the man from Bonfebba," or "the spirit priestess of Mehanna," or the "cousin of the blacksmith." To a reader in the United States, United Kingdom, or France, such expression may seem quite stilted. When I wrote *The Sorcerer's Burden*, a novel, I tried to replicate the formality of Songhay speech, which provoked the following response from a young hotshot literary agent in New York City.

> . . . read much of your book, and I wanted to be in touch. Fact is, I think the idea, the setting, the story here is really awesome. Really interesting and different and intense. But if I'm honest, I think there are a few problems that became big issues for me. I think Omar's tone is meticulous and perfect, but he speaks in the same way he thinks, which is dry and lacking of emotion, and then, everyone else speaks in the same way, polite and careful and it feels like there's only one voice all the way through, which is pretty hard for me. If the dialogue had more spark to it, more interactiveness and individuality, I think this book could be really, really great. I know this is just me, others might think differently, but I'll tell you—I don't write comments like this unless I think there's merit. So I do wish you the best of luck, Paul.[24]

Although I didn't like his decision about my book, the comments convinced me to seek a middle ground in my dialogue writing, which, in the end, made the novel more accessible to a broader audience of readers.

It is always good to read masterful dialogue. In what follows I present dialogue from Walter Mosley, a master of dialogue in fiction; Joshua Hammer, who presents memorable dialogue in creative nonfiction; Ruth Behar, one of our finest ethnographers, who knows how to construct powerful dialogue; and the incomparable

Zora Neale Hurston, the legendary ethnographer and folklorist who masterfully employed dialogue to set a scene or craft character.

Walter Mosley writes fabulous crime novels. The major protagonist who appears in many of his books is Easy Rawlins, an African American private detective who knows a thing or two because he's seen a thing or two. In Mosley novels the plots and characterizations are often articulated through dialogue. Here's a short example from his 2005 novel, *Cinnamon Kiss*, which features a conversation between Easy Rawlins and Cynthia Aubec:

> "Hi. My name is Ezekiel Rawlins." I held out my hand.
>
> A big grin came across her but somehow the mirth didn't make it to her eyes. She shook my hand.
>
> "How can I help you?"
>
> "I'm a private detective from down in L.A.," I said. "I've been hired to find a woman named Philomena Cargill . . . by her family."
>
> "Cinnamon," the woman said without hesitation. "Axel's friend."
>
> "That's Axel Bowers?"
>
> "Yes. He's my partner here."
>
> She looked around the storefront. I did too.
>
> "Not a very lucrative business," I speculated.
>
> The woman laughed. It was a real laugh.
>
> "That depends on what you see as profit, Mr. Rawlins. Axel and I are committed to helping the poor people of society get a fair shake from the legal system."
>
> "You're both lawyers?"
>
> "Yes," she said. "I got my degree from UCLA and Axel got his across the Bay in Berkeley. I worked for the state for a while but didn't feel very good about that. When Axel asked me to join him, I jumped at the chance."
>
> "What's your name?" I asked.
>
> "Oh. Excuse my manners. My name is Cynthia Aubec."
>
> "French?"
>
> "I was born in Canada," she said. "Montreal."[25]

Notice how Mosley's dialogue contains both speech and descriptive action, both of which lend themselves to the flow of the interaction.

The second example is a dialogue from Joshua Hammer's stunning work of creative nonfiction, *The Bad-Ass Librarians of Timbuktu*, which describes how a Timbuktu guardian of his family's collection of ancient manuscripts saved those irreplaceable texts from the fires of radical Islamists who had sacked and occupied his fabled city. Here is a conversation between Haidara, the protagonist of Hammer's book, and some Libyan officials, representing Muammar al-Gaddafi. After looking through the manuscripts the Libyan officials wanted to buy the collection.

> "We have a proposition for you," they said.
> "I'm listening," Haidara replied.
> "We want to buy everything we see here." They opened a briefcase, and showed Haidara stacks of bills in various currencies. . . .
> "Thanks, but no thanks," he told the Libyans. "You never said that you were coming here to attempt to purchase the manuscripts."
> "What do you mean? We will pay you in any currency you want."
> "It's not for sale."
> "Why not?"
> "Because this isn't for me. This is the heritage of Mali. It belongs to a great nation."
> "But we can make you comfortable for the rest of your life."
> "No," he said.[26]

Here again, the dialogue underscores the rhythm of a tense interaction between Haidara, the central character of the work, and the cash-carrying Libyan officials.

A third example is from Ruth Behar's classic ethnographic memoir, *The Vulnerable Observer*. The conversation is between Polonia, Rufi, and Behar and takes place in rural Spain. The topic is how to shroud a cadaver.

Polonia began: "When it was my mother, we [she and her sister] shrouded her. And Junta. She died at night, at four, at three or so in the morning. We shrouded her between the three of us my sister Junta and I. Florencia [her brother-in-law] was here, too, my husband was also here, which was curious, it was fiesta—"

Rufi interrupted her to ask a generalizing question. "But how did you wash them?"

Her mother shrugged. "You wash them."

"With a towel, a sponge?"

"You wash them very well. No, nothing, it doesn't mean anything, because it is a normal body."

Rufi, playing the ethnographer, offers an explanation. "Why do you wash them, so that they will be clean when they go to heaven?" Rufi's zeal to interpret and draw conclusions—perhaps because it offers too close a mirror of me in ethnographic costume—makes me cringe in my seat.

"I don't know. These are customs."

Rufi turns to me and says: "It's folkloric, isn't it, Ruth?"

I, trying my best, intercept with a snatch of information I have picked up from an old will. "Yes, customs. Sometimes they dress them up in nun's or monk's clothes."[27]

In this short dialogue the reader learns something about not only mortuary customs in rural Spain but also the tangled complexities of the ethnographer's subject position in the field.

The final dialogue example comes from Zora Neale Hurston's classic work, *Mules and Men*. Consider how Hurston uses dialogue to establish immediately a sense of place, her childhood home in Eatonville, Florida, as it was in 1927. She arrives in Eatonville in a car. After describing a group of men playing Florida-flip on the porch of store, the following dialogue takes place.

"Hello, boys," I hailed them as I went into neutral.

They looked up from the game and for a moment it looked as if they had forgotten me. Then B. Moseley said: "Well, if it ain't Zora

Hurston." Then everybody crowded around the car to help greet me.

"You gointer stay awhile, Zora?"

"Yep. Several months."

"Where you gointer stay, Zora?"

"With Mett and Ellis, I reckon."

"Mett" was Mrs. Armetta Jones, an intimate friend of mine since childhood and Ellis was her husband. Their house stands under the huge camphor tree on the front street.

"Hello, heart-string," Mayor Hiram Lester yelled as he hurried up the street. "We heard all about you up north. You back home for good, I hope."

"Nope, Ah come to collect some old stories and tales and Ah know y'all know plenty of 'em and that's why Ah headed straight for home."

"What you mean, Zora, them big old lies we tell when we're jus' sittin' around here on the store porch doin' nothin," asked B. Moseley.[28]

In artful ethnography the crafting of character complements the evocation of space/place and dialogue. All too often the people in ethnographies remain obscure. What do they look like? What physical features do they possess that distinguish them from other people? Might it be the way their faces are set in a frown, a grimace, or a grin? How do they hold themselves? Do they walk rapidly with a stiff-legged gait, or do they skip or limp? Are they unsteady on their feet? Do they have a distinctive way of speaking? Do they repeat a phrase regularly, a phrase that is a window into their state of being? When readers have read an ethnographic text, will they remember the people described in the book? In artful ethnography sensuous words evoke the idiosyncrasies of character to create an alluring and hard-to-forget portrait. Here are some brief portraits from Michael Chabon's novel, *Wonder Boys*, from Anna Badkhen's book on Fulani transhumance, *Walking with Abel*, and Gina Athena Ulysse's book, *Because When God Is Too Busy: Haiti, Me, and the World.*

In *Wonder Boys*, Grady Tripp, a prodigy novelist, suffering from writer's block, goes to the airport to meet his famous literary agent, Terry Crabtree.

> "Tripp," said Crabtree, approaching me with his free hand extended. He reached up with both arms to embrace me and I held on to him for an extra second or two, tightly, trying to determine from the soundness of his ribs whether he loved me still. "Good to see you. How are you?"
>
> I let go of him and took a step backward. He wore the usual Crabtree expression of scorn, and his eyes were bright and hard, but he didn't look as though he were angry with me. He'd been letting his hair grow long as he got older, not, as is the case with some fashionable men in their forties, in compensation for any incipient baldness, but out of a vanity more pure and unchallengeable: he had beautiful hair, thick and chestnut-colored and falling in a flawless curtain to his shoulders. He was wearing a well-cut olive-drab belted raincoat over a handsome suit—an Italian number in a metallic silk that was green like the back of a dollar bill—a pair of woven leather loafers without socks, and round schoolboy spectacles I'd never seen before.[29]

In *Walking with Abel*, Anna Badkhen describes Fanta, a rural Fulani woman in Mali.

> Fanta nestled the calabashes on top of her head and set off on the southbound path toward Wereka. She did no farewells; this was a ritual she performed every other day and it did not merit ceremony. Nor did she ease gradually into her walk. She started right out of the camp at a quick steady stride that never changed until she reached the village. It was the tempo of her last walk, and of her walks before that, and of her mother's, and of all the milkmaids' past recall who had fixed their footsteps to the trail before. She

simply picked it up. She would have picked up a dropped calabash that way, or a grindstone she had loaned to a neighbor.

At first Fanta walked with her right hand raised to hold the straw lids so the wind wouldn't blow them away. After a hundred paces the arm and wrist drained of blood and began to ache. She stopped and shook off her right plastic flipflop and with her toes scooped up from the ground a flat stone. She flexed the right leg at the knee and stood on her left unbending leg and without leaning, without looking, reached behind her with her right arm and picked the stone out of her foot. Neck perfectly straight the calabashes steady on her head. She had done this a thousand times before. Her bubble-printed shawl flapped against her cheek. She placed the rock on the topmost lid and let both arms fall like a marionette's arms by her sides and walked again. Around her ankles night moisture rose cold from the drying fields. Pied crows hopped in low labyrinths of manure.[30]

Gina Athena Ulysse is an anthropologically trained artist-poet who crafts character in a particularly powerful way. Consider what this passage about the will to speak says about a person and the context that shapes her character.

> **Her Silence:** And if her rage remains unspoken, unexpressed, then, what becomes of it? One too many have pontificated on the enigmatic mad white woman relegated to the attic. She who dared to question social mores that incarcerated her or turned her into wallpaper. Less is known of the black female rage. There is usually no place for it. Its very articulation regardless of how much politesse is another death sentence or better punishment for those uncontrollable REMEMORIES bound to stay crushed to her body, her archive. She dares not speak. Shut your mouth. SHHHHHH . . . Careful. There is no place for unruly girls like you who do not know when to be quiet. Shhhhhhhhhhhhhh. . . . When not to offend white sensibilities. When not to choke. Swallow. When to submit. Shhhhhhhhhhhhhhhhhhhhh—Take a deep breath. Swallow . . . Swallow . . . Swallow . . . There is no safe word.[31]

In these examples character is constructed through the physical description of faces, movements, dress, internal and external speech, and space. It is also constructed through what is said and unsaid, what is stated and what is left to the reader's imagination.

Whenever I visited Paris, I tried to sit in on screenings in Jean Rouch's projection room, which was above his cluttered offices on the second floor of the Musée de l'Homme. When young filmmakers arranged to show Rouch, a legendary twentieth-century documentarian, one of their unfinished films, he would routinely invite commentary from a motley assortment of people—scholars, other filmmakers, an occasional patron of the museum, and one or two students.

"But I don't know anything about film," one of the invitees once said at one of the screening sessions.

"That's good," Rouch replied. "It doesn't matter."

After the projection, Rouch, who always sat in the front row, turned around, faced his invitees, and facilitated an impassioned debate on film technicalities, sound quality, editing techniques, and postproduction problems. The person who had proclaimed her ignorance of film found the film "uninspiring."

Rouch then began to ask questions that I had heard before.

"Where is the story in this film?"

"How can you fix the story?"

"What can you do so that the film connects with the audience?"[32]

For Jean Rouch story was always prior to theory. That is not to say that theories are not useful and important. They are. It is to say that in the world of science, theories, given the instabilities of scientific truths, have short shelf lives. In the wake of erstwhile theories, though, we seem to always come back to the story, the foundation of the ethnographic record, which is the anthropological gift to the world. The narratives that comprise the ethnographic record are texts and films that can, if they are well crafted, remain open to the world. As Jean Rouch well knew, stories create a bond between the filmmaker and the audience or the author and her or his readers. Through the power of evocation stories can move us to think new thoughts, construct new realities, and feel new feelings.[33] They are the catalyst for social change. In his book, *The Storytelling Animal*, Jonathan Gottschall captures well the power of narrative. He writes: "Story—sacred and profane—is perhaps the main cohering force in human life. A society is composed of fractious people with different personalities, goals, and agendas. What connects us beyond our kinship ties? Story . . . Story is the counterforce to social disorder, the tendency of things to fall apart. Story is the center without which the rest cannot hold."[34] Indeed, stories are windows through which we encounter the human condition. They demonstrate how we are all connected. That is the power of the story. That is the work of art in ethnography.

So how do you learn to craft a good story?

Why are some films and/or ethnographic texts more memorable than others?

Maurice Merleau-Ponty and Michael Jackson might say that memorable ethnographies are the ones in which the sensuous projection of image—in prose and film—compels an audience to sense the drama of social life. Stories that poetically showcase the lived and unlived environment, that feature idiosyncratic dialogue, and that underscore the vulnerabilities of character have the capacity to create connections between authors and audiences. They have the capacity to remain "open to the world."

But in the art of ethnography, there is something more profoundly existential at play. Songhay elders love to recite the following proverb: *Kumba hinka ga charotarey numey* (It takes two hands to nourish a friendship). Indeed, the sensuous evocation of space, dialogue, and character present a necessary but not sufficient condition for crafting the kind of stories that comprise an artful ethnography. In the end, the artistic quality of ethnography devolves less from technique and more from how you live your life. Do you live in the moment? Do you walk with confidence on your path? Do you "open your ears" and listen to elders? Are you willing to enter the stressful arena of representational vulnerability? These life choices implicate ethnographers among their others and enable them to tell a good story. For me, the depth, texture, and staying power of an ethnographic film or ethnographic text emerges directly from the depth of the relationships that the ethnographer has developed. No matter the sophistication of technical practice or philosophical nuance, this deceptively simple principle sets the foundation for the future of an artful ethnography the insights of which chart a course for confronting the social turbulence of a troubled world. As scholars, is it not our obligation to artfully recount these insightful stories to sweeten the human condition?

It takes two hands to nourish a friendship.

Wisdom from the Edge is not an attempt to tell the reader how to write a good story or a memorable ethnography. It is a book in which I try to show the reader some of the expository elements that make for a good story or a memorable book. In the early chapters I attempt to balance "telling" and "showing" to weave a narrative tapestry—a weaving of the world. In succeeding chapters I attempt to explore the senses to "show" readers a way to articulate complex ethnographic data evocatively and provocatively.[35] The chapters, then, are laced with sensuous descriptions and narratives crafted to compel the reader to turn the page and to eventually engage in what Richard Rorty long ago called "edifying conversation." In chapter 1, "Imaging Knowledge: Artful Vision in Slow Research," I evoke the sense of sight—the creation of images—to suggest one path toward a more artful ethnography. In chapter 2, "In the Shade of the Jujube Tree," I conjure the senses of sight, sound, and smell to describe the slow epistemology of West African divination. The sensory description of Songhay spirit possession is the subject of chapter 3. Here I demonstrate how smell, sound, and vision become integral ingredients in recipes of and for spirit possession. In chapter 4, "Tasting Harmony in the World," I consider the oft-neglected senses of smell and taste to demonstrate how they can shape the texture of (Songhay) social relations.

The capacity of art to express powerfully the ineffable and the peripheral is considered in chapter 5, "Peripheral Knowledge and the Imponderables of the Between." How can one use artfully evocative prose to represent experience that defies reductive explanation? Chapter 6, "The World According to Rouch," is a step-by-step exploration of the filmmaker Jean Rouch's view of the world and how it ensured his artful and moving representation of others. In chapter 7, "Wisdom from the Edge of the Village," I describe how an artful approach to ethnographic representation is particularly important in perilous times. Writing sensuously evocative prose, I suggest, is a powerfully effective way to communicate anthropological insights to the public. In the end, those accessible insights can make social life a bit sweeter for us all.

Part I

THE SENSES IN ARTFUL ETHNOGRAPHY

We are the mirror
As well as the face in it.
We are tasting the taste this minute
of eternity. We are the pain
and what causes the pain, both. We are the
sweet cold water and the jar that pours

Rumi

1

Imaging Knowledge

ARTFUL VISION IN SLOW RESEARCH

Andurnya kala suuru
"Life is patience"

Songhay saying

N'da suuru go ni se, ni fonda ga feri
"If you are patient, your path will open"

Songhay proverb

The straight highway lies before us, but we cannot
take it because it is permanently closed.

Wittgenstein, Philosophical Investigations

Speed and expediency shape much of our contemporary learning. We tend to move quickly from subject to subject. Representations can be rapidly downloaded, scanned, reproduced, perused, edited, and reconfigured—all to increase human understanding and connection. But as the philosopher Mark Taylor and social psychologist Sherry Turkle have suggested, the culture of speed, which has positively increased the spread of information, has also brought increases in social disconnection, eroded interpersonal empathy, and limited processes of thinking.[1] There is no shortage of philosophical works that offer alternative approaches to living in the *culture of speed*. Having long conducted fieldwork in West Africa, I believe that one alternative to the culture of speed is embodied in the wisdom of people like the Songhay of Niger and Mali. But can the wisdom of a non-Western culture offer ways to increase human connection, enhance interpersonal empathy, and deepen contemplative thinking?

In this chapter I suggest that the production of visual imagery shows us a powerfully ethical way—through sensuous narrative and shared anthropology—to practice slowly produced artful ethnography in a fast world. Here I examine the work and practices of two great visual anthropologists, Jean Rouch and Lisbet Holtedahl. The research methodology and filmic strategies of these master anthropologists, I suggest, have been profoundly shaped by the slow epistemology of the Songhay (Rouch) and Fulani (Holtedahl) peoples of West Africa. Indeed, the visual narratives and filmic practices of Rouch and Holtedahl demonstrate powerfully the rewards of slowly developed storytelling and image making. Their works underscore the intellectual gifts of taking a slow path toward the production of knowledge. Their films show us how to move forcefully and ethically into the anthropological future, which may help reinforce our humanity and heal the world.

Imagine the following scene. Sometime in the early 1980s you are in Paris. You enter the Musée de l'Homme. You climb a steep flight of marble stairs and turn toward a temporary partition that shields a small opening that leads to Jean Rouch's Comité du Film Ethnographique office, which is abuzz with activity. Rouch sits behind a cluttered desk, perched on a platform that commands the office. He is somehow simultaneously talking on the phone and debating some bureaucratic detail with his erstwhile associate, Françoise Foucault. Tacked up haphazardly on the wall are countless photos of famous documentarians, filmmakers, and actors. There are scores of boxes filled with photographs. Along the stairs that lead up to a second floor, you might stumble upon piles of haphazardly arranged metal cans containing many of Rouch's finished and unfinished films.

Amid this organized chaos, Rouch hangs up the phone and asks everyone to climb the stairs to his projection room. Some young documentarians have come to Paris to project their unfinished work to the master. They are nervous.

As they project their film, they wonder: what will he think?

There is heated debate about film strategies and editing techniques.

In time, Rouch chimes in. He wants to know more about the texture of the film's story.

Rouch's focus on the story during this and every other projection room session I attended cuts to the heart of his project—the art of storytelling, the importance of which he learned from his Songhay mentors in the Republics of Niger and Mali. For them, deep knowledge is conveyed through narrative, which has the capacity to evoke complexity through the elegant simplicity of stories. The power of the story, Rouch taught me, emerges not just from the tale that is told but from the more profound context of longstanding friendship and trust—shared anthropology. Jean Rouch's oeuvre also demonstrates that like indigenous elders, scholars and filmmakers are the custodians of knowledge. As custodians, the most important obligation is to tell stories that convey this cherished knowledge to the next generation. These principles, which are evoked in Jean Rouch's films and texts, are the bedrock of Songhay epistemology and the foundation of Songhay wisdom. It takes time and patience for the mind to develop, for practices to be refined, for a person to take full command of her or his work.

And once that full command is achieved, the elder's greatest obligation is to pass the knowledge on to the next generation.[2]

You stand before the entrance to Sultan Issa Maigari's vast palace, an imposing image. Then you move inside the palace's dark

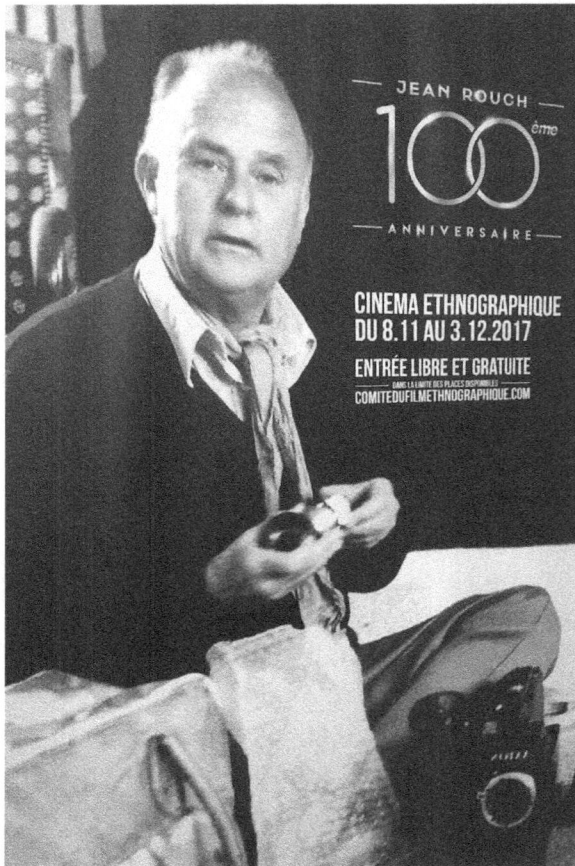

FIGURE 2
Poster of the Jean Rouch Centennial Celebration. ©Paul Stoller.

corridors and find the sultan, dressed in a splendidly embroidered purple robe, making his way through the dark sinewy corridors. He sees one of his young toddlers and picks him up. Together they move toward the light of the inner courtyard. In the distance you see a team of women cleaning the compound with whisks fashioned from dried grass. Beyond the women, you see the sultan's magnificent black stallion. Courtiers prepare the horse for the sultan, who will ride it into the center of Ngaoundere to meet the Cameroonian minister of the interior—the juxtaposition of the traditional and the modern and a sign of irrevocable change. As the sultan approaches his horse, court musicians, in tribute to their ruler, blow their trumpets. The sultan mounts his horse. Surrounded by an entourage of courtiers, Sultan Issa Maigari slowly makes his way to the center of town, all symbolic of the long-standing religious and political prestige of the royal ruler. This slow take in Lisbet Holtedahl's *The Sultan's Burden*[3] underscores the slow pace of everyday life—even in the royal enclaves of the Northern Cameroon Adamawa Sultanate. This scene depicts life as it has been lived in this faraway place— or does it?

When Holtedahl's camera takes us deep into the corridors of Sultan Issa Maigari's palace, viewers get a complex portrait of the sultan, who is the spiritual and political leader of the Adamawa Province of Northern Cameroon. He is sauntering slowly among his wives, his children, his advisors, and his praise singers. It is an intimate glimpse—the result of years of shared anthropology— into the character of a proud, traditional leader who has the daunting challenge of confronting the irrevocable loss of prestige as the Cameroonian state begins the process of secular democratization. The film evokes a profoundly human theme: what are the existential dimensions of love and loss?

In her latest production, *Wives*, which was filmed between 1992 and 2015, Holtedahl brings her slow and shared anthropology into the compound of an Islamic scholar, El Hajji Alkali Ibrahim Goni, who was for forty-five years a traditional judge in the sultanate of Issa Maigari.[4] The film showcases the uneven textures of relations between El Hajji and his many wives, some of whom he divorced, some of whom died, and some of whom he divorced and remarried. In Holtedahl's words, the film describes the "various household scenes of everyday life events and interviews. With this, I hope to identify the audio-visual material's contribution to my understanding of marriage, love, and dependency of six of El Hajji's wives and their husband."[5] At the end of the film El Hajji Goni, tired and old, is approaching death. From this intimate inside perspective the audience sees how the spread of death's shadow brings into stark relief El Hajji Goni's humanity and his deep-seated feelings of love and loss in a household far removed from our experience. In so doing, Holtedahl makes the strange familiar, using slow and shared anthropology to create emotional and social connections in an increasingly disconnected world.

These intimate and deeply human films are the result of Lisbet Holtedahl's gradually developed shared anthropology. Like Jean Rouch among the Songhay, Holtedahl spent decades of field time among the Fulani of Northern Cameroon. She learned to speak fluent Fulfulde, which enabled her to cultivate long-standing friendships with a wide variety of people in the region. In time this slow approach enhanced her sensitivity to the human dilemmas of her subjects, which, in turn, has given her films, like those of Rouch, an uncanny tenderness, a seductive informality and no small measure of pathos.

FIGURE 3
Lisbet Holtedahl filming in the field. © Trond Waage.

If scholars commit to doing long-term fieldwork, a commitment that spans many decades, they become sensitive to the accountability of their work. How will the people they have described in articles, books, and films respond to one's professional work? Will they understand it? Will anthropological texts and images misrepresent them? Will they offend them? These issues, of course, have long been of deep anthropological concern—especially so now that social media makes anthropological work so much more accessible to the represented. Like physicians most contemporary anthropologists subscribe to the healer's oath: do no harm. And yet, despite the best of efforts, medical procedures sometimes inadvertently do a great deal of harm. The same, of course, can be said of anthropological essays, ethnographies, and ethnographic films.

This issue is of particular importance in visual anthropology—especially in turbulent times. Through social media, images travel far and wide. They sometimes unintentionally project scenes that reinforce primitivist and racist ideologies. In 1992 Wilton Martinez's classic essay "Who Constructs Anthropological Knowledge?" demonstrated the pervasiveness of the misinterpretation of ethnographic visual images. Based on surveys of ethnographic film audiences, Martinez found that many ethnographic films—even well-known classics—have tended to reinforce primitivist stereotypes, the very worst spectator outcome an anthropologist might experience. Martinez "found many students decode films in an 'aberrant' way (Eco, 1979) with relatively high levels of disinterest, 'culture shock' and/or alienation, and with a relatively low level of 'understanding' (correspondent with textual and pedagogical intended meanings."[6] These inconvenient findings mean that scholars, especially image-making anthropologists, need to take care as they come to terms with arenas of negative audience interpretations.

In contemporary anthropology, then, representational challenges are monumental. If you are a writer, how do you craft a faithful and representative text in which readers are inspired to read on? For the filmmaker, how do you lure the audience into a sensuous visual world in a way that does not reinforce destructive stereotypes? For great practitioners like Jean Rouch and Lisbet Holtedahl the answer, which is consistent with Martinez's findings about the *readability* of narrative films, is deceptively simple: one entices audiences with stories gleaned from slowly developed friendships that are full of love and loss. The texture of an essay or film, then, devolves from the quality of the social connections between the anthropologist and the people he or she attempts to represent.

Taking his cue from the film practices of Robert Flaherty, who, in search of collaborative input, showed his unfinished films to his Inuit subjects, Jean Rouch decided early on to make collaborative films among the Songhay and Dogon of Niger and Mali. For more than thirty years, he collaborated with his Nigerien sidekicks— Damouré Zika, Lam Ibrahim, and Tallou Mouzourane—to make films that joyously celebrated the often-inexplicable complexities of ever-changing social life in West Africa. In a film practice grounded in his long-standing friendships with Nigeriens, Rouch always concerned himself with the audience. He often talked about three audiences. He liked to say: I am the first audience. Does the film work for me? The second audience is composed of the people in front of the camera. What do the subjects think about the film? Is it faithful to their lived reality? The third group is the broader public. What can the film teach people about the human condition? If all three audiences like a work, Rouch would say, the film "will give birth to other films."

In the early 1950s Jean Rouch had footage of what was to become *Bataille sur le grand fleuve*, a film about the great hippopotamus hunters of Firgoun, Niger.[7] Rouch brought the unfinished footage of the hippo hunt to Ayoru, a Niger River market town, near Firgoun. He nailed a sheet to a mud brick wall and, using a portable generator, projected his footage. The Firgoun hippo hunters silently watched the projection. When Rouch asked for comments, the Firgoun hunters, who immediately understood the language of film, critiqued what they had seen, objected to the background stock music that, like an invisible intruder, accompanied the hunters on their quest. They said that noise (*cosongo*, in Songhay) would spoil the hunt. Accordingly, Rouch removed the background music from his film.[8]

Like Rouch, Holtedahl's shared anthropology compelled her to become profoundly sensitive to local responses to her work. In their essay on these issues, Arntsen and Holtedahl wrote.

> Our preoccupation with the recipient should be seen mainly as a result of many years' preoccupation with the impact on society of research-based knowledge. Our engagement with film and our attempts to create and disseminate knowledge by use of film as a tool have proved to be very useful for such an appreciation. When analyzing the situatedness of knowledge and focusing on the person who is supposed to "receive" "the knowledge," it is necessary to differentiate possible positions of the receiver. When anthropologists are in the field interacting with local "informants," i.e. with their research partners, they have notions about who will be their target groups. They see themselves processing material for future dissemination. The target group persons have qualities and interests. We think these notions are relevant for the anthropologists' observations and behaviour. But the research partners, too, have their target groups: First of all, they are each other's audience in the social situations. In addition, they are often conscious of other audiences or target groups with which they are more or less familiar: the future readers of the anthropologists' book and viewers of his/her film.[9]

Audiences of people who have been in front of the camera, of course, have their own subjective interpretations of what they are seeing. As Arntsen and Holtedahl suggest, anthropologists should take these issues very seriously—a consequence of slowly developed shared anthropology.

Even if scholars carefully anticipate many of the negative reactions to their works and take care to craft a good story, there is still no guarantee that a text or film will resonate with readers or audiences. There are books and films that hit all the right notes—good stories, sensuous descriptions, breathtaking cinematography, and seamless editing—but somehow remain obscure, unread, unwatched, or uninspiring.

What is missing from these books and films?

One potential answer might be the presence of characters who are vulnerable—imperfect human beings whose life stories compel readers or audiences to connect. In his films Jean Rouch understood this important element of storytelling. In Rouch's *Jaguar*, the audience meets four young Nigeriens, each with his own set of social problems, who must confront the challenge of their times—earning wage labor or entrepreneurial profits in the Colonial Gold Coast to help their struggling families in Niger. On their epic journey through today's Burkina Faso, Togo, and Ghana, they stumble here and there. In a variety of tense and funny scenes, they reveal their prejudices and express their wonder of the new. Through extraordinary bricolage, they somehow make their way to Kumasi where they open a small shop, *Petit a petit l'oiseaux fair son nid* (Little by little the bird makes its nest). They sell *nyama-nyama* (a little of this and a little of that) and make money. As I have witnessed countless times, audiences in Niger, Europe, and North America follow the protagonists with intense interest. Against all odds, they save enough money to bring home the bounty of their exotic mission to the edge of the world. Upon their return they heroically give away all that they had earned. Indeed, in his innovative films of ethno-fiction (*Jaguar*, *La pyramid humaine*, *Moi, un noir*, and not to forget *Chronique d'un été*) Rouch showcases vulnerable characters—men and women, old and young, West Africans, and French. Within and between the frames of these classic films, these vulnerable characters open their being to the world. They invite viewers to enter their complicated worlds. Their poignant stories connect viewers to a different set of insights that are unveiled in a new world. In my experience, audiences tend to accept this invitation and learn something new.[10]

It takes time and patient persistence to evoke the complexities of character in a text or film, a lesson well gleaned from Lisbet Holtedahl's recent film, *Wives*, for which Holtedahl brought her slow and shared anthropology into the compound of the previously mentioned Islamic scholar, El Hajji Alkali Ibrahim Goni, the traditional judge in the Adamawa Sultanate of Issa Maigari. Through events and interviews the film describes scenes of everyday household life. Through image making Holtedahl enhances our comprehension of the intimate twists and turns of marriage, love, and dependency in El Hajji's compound. Toward the end of the film a visibly ill El Hajji Goni opens himself to the audience. Viewers learn of his triumphs, his disappointments, his pride of craft, and his personal remorse. In the face of death his dignity draws the audience to him and compels viewers to remember him—a model for us all.

To embrace vulnerability is a risky proposition. It violates what Mary Louise Pratt long ago called "conventions of representation."[11] For his part Rouch invented a new genre, ethno-fiction, to underscore the vulnerabilities of men and women confronting the decay of West African colonialism, the irrevocable change brought on by independence, and the ugly persistence of racism—themes that are still very much with us in the world. For her part, Holtedahl took such time and care in her fieldwork that a Fulani cleric allowed her camera of intimacy to record his most private moments and his most deeply guarded emotions, and this among a people known for their deep reserve and rectitude.[12] You could say that Rouch and Holtedahl went *rogue* in their films to depict human vulnerabilities, depictions that move audiences to engage in a powerfully silent Buberian I-Thou dialogue—a powerful way to promote meaningful change.[13]

Authors of ethnographic works that remain open to the world try to make sure that human emotion and vulnerability are fore-grounded in the text or showcased within and between the frames of films. Following the epistemological path of wise Songhay and Fulani elders, Rouch and Holtedahl practiced slow anthropology well before the invention of the slow food movement, which was initially a protest of the opening of a McDonald's, the icon of fast-food establishments, near the Spanish Steps in Rome.[14]

The discipline of anthropology, of course, is well suited to fit into the ever-expanding matrix of slowness. As the visual ethnographic practices of Jean Rouch and Lisbet Holtedahl demonstrate, anthropology has the distinction of being a slow science in a fast world. It takes many years to develop anthropological insights—years spent listening to the people anthropologists encounter in the field. This slow practice has produced the ethnographic record, an invaluable body of knowledge that underscores the wisdom of others, a wisdom that we would be wise to extend to the social, cultural, and political infelicities that constitute our contemporary culture of speed.

Practicing a slow ethnography, however, is more than taking your time to conduct long-term field research and then carefully crafting books and films; it is also about the gradual maturation of knowledge. Jean Rouch learned this principle from Songhay elders in the Republic of Niger who have long understood the power of slowness. In my own education, these kind and patient elders insisted that as a young man I first learn the rudimentary elements of sorcerous knowledge. They forced me to slow down. "That's enough talk for now," they would tell me on my visits to Niger. "Come back next year," they would instruct me, "to continue to learn."

"But I want to learn more," I'd tell my teachers with no small amount of impatience.

"You're not ready yet," they'd say. "Come back next year."

My apprenticeship with Adamu Jenitongo spanned seventeen years. Toward the end of his life, he told me: "You have lived among us for a long time, but to understand us you must grow old with us."

When my mentor's death brought an end to my apprenticeship, I thought I had learned a great deal. As time passed by, I realized that despite my seventeen-year apprenticeship to a Songhay elder, my comprehension of things Songhay lacked depth.

In the slow world of Songhay sorcery, I found that illness is a great teacher. My experience of a life-threatening illness challenged me to see myself more clearly. It sensitized me to the pain and suffering of others. It compelled me to understand that a person's greatest obligation—as a healer or as a scholar—is to pass slowly acquired knowledge on to the next generation. In so doing the sorcerers, scholars, filmmakers, and anthropologists open themselves to the world. In so doing they are likely to find the resolve to invent a new genre, like Jean Rouch, to make profoundly intimate films like Lisbet Holtedahl, or to understand how a confrontation with serious illness might compel a person to return to where he or she began and, to paraphrase T. S. Eliot, know the place for the first time.[15]

Artful ethnographers can produce texts and films that are more likely to be long read, seen, and debated. More than fifty years after they first appeared, Jean Rouch's films continue to underscore the fragility of human being. They teach us about ugliness, hatred, and the courage of the oppressed. Lisbet Holtedahl's films evoke profound dignity in the face of love and loss, themes that connect us all.

Beyond the theoretical flavor of the day, anthropology's great gift to the world is the ethnographic record, which through artfully constructed prose narrative or film image can forge memorable bonds between writers and their readers, and between filmmakers and their audiences. These slowly developed bonds take us a step closer to a more convivial present. Jean Rouch and Lisbet Holtedahl have walked this slow path toward knowledge. It is a way filled with respect for the lessons of the elders whose paths lead to wisdom. It is a path well worth taking, as I attempt to demonstrate in chapter 2, which explores the deliberately slow, highly personal, and decidedly sensuous path one takes to learn about divination in rural Niger.

2

In the Shade of the Jujube Tree

Kwaara banda daarey, yeow s'a gar.
"The stranger will never encounter the sweet jujube
tree behind the village."

Songhay proverb

Among the Songhay people of Niger and Mali, there are prov-
erbs that speak to the relationship of strangers to the children
of the village. Strangers are welcomed. They may live in the village,
but even if they stay for years, the children of the village, or the
kwaar'izey, tend to regard them as transitory figures. Sooner or
later, the stranger will return home. As Songhay people like to say:
Yeow harendang no nda a mana bia, a ga weyma (Strangers are
like the mist. If they are not gone by morning, they will be by afternoon). As transitory figures, strangers may learn a great deal about
social life in a community, but it is not likely that they will ever
discover the sweetest elements of the village. They will not find the
elusive jujube tree. In the end, they are not likely to understand
fully the most important elements of village life.[1]

Sometimes a stranger is lucky enough to stumble upon the jujube
tree. During the many years I lived among the Songhay people of
Niger, I learned about the rhythm of everyday life in rural villages.

I had the good fortune to become an apprentice to Songhay healers who taught me about medicinal herbs and healing rituals. As a man living in a society in which everyday activities are gender segregated, I did not learn much about the private lives of women—until I had the opportunity to meet and befriend Fatouma Seyni.

On a hot morning walk through the small village where I had been living for some time, I heard the clacks of pestles thumping mortars. Following the sound, I stopped at the entrance of a compound. As was customary, I clapped three times. Someone invited me in. I entered the compound, an open rectangular space of dirt with a central well, several scraggly acacias, and a tallish jujube tree, all partially set off by a fence fashioned from millet stalks. In the jujube's shade, I saw four women pounding millet seeds. They stopped working and stared at me.

One of the women waved at me and pointed to an overturned mortar. Given the rarity of male strangers being asked to join Songhay women, the invitation surprised and pleased me. As I sat down on the mortar, the women continued with their work. They talked and laughed and pounded their pestles, slowly transforming millet seeds into flour.

"Do you pound every day?" I asked, awkwardly trying to make conversation.

The women laughed. "Of course, we do. If we didn't pound millet, no one would eat," said the woman who had invited me into the compound.

She held herself straight and erect. It was difficult to guess her age, but her face had deep lines. She had beautiful, large, clear brown eyes that twinkled in the morning sunlight. She had heard about the white stranger living among them and asked why I wanted to spend time in a remote place like Mehanna.

"I want to get to know the lives of the people here."

"Few men want to join women as they work," she said, "but if you like you can sit and listen to our stories."

I told her that I would be very honored to listen.

"I am Fatouma Seyni," she said.

Fatouma Seyni became my friend and one of my Songhay mentors, a person who eventually taught me about the mysteries of

FIGURE 4
Fatouma Seyni, master diviner of Mehanna, Niger. © Paul Stoller.

Songhay divination. In her quiet manner she exemplified the grace and dignity of many of the Songhay women I gradually came to know over the years. Fatouma had a patient manner that guided my development as a scholar and my maturity as a human being. I am forever grateful to have been lucky enough to befriend a group of West African elders, men and women, who patiently taught me about, magic, divination, the healing property of plants, individual vulnerability, the human capacity for resilience, and, not least, the importance of acknowledging how love and loss shape the human condition.

This chapter is an homage to Fatouma Seyni. In it, I follow the senses of smell and taste to weave threads of narrative and ethnography into a tapestry that evokes the profundity of West African practical wisdom. I like to say that I sit on the shoulders of my West African mentors. Much of what I have written is a testament to the foundation they set for me. And yet, my path, which emerges from their thoughts and practices, is not their path. The foundation they set marked a beginning, not an end.

As the Songhay elders like to say: "You cannot walk where there is no ground."[2]

Holding on to her pestle, Fatouma Seyni introduced me to the other women in her compound—Hampsa, Mariama, and Jitu, all younger family members. At first, the women hesitated to talk in the presence of a man, especially a white man. Slowly they became less reticent. I sat quietly, listening to them talk about family life in Mehanna—unfaithful husbands, food shortages, sick children, conflict among co-wives in polygynous households, the life of women between husbands.

Not wishing to overstay my welcome, I said goodbye after a little more than an hour of listening. I was surprised and honored when

Fatouma invited me to visit again. I began to stop by once or twice a week during my morning walk. The women gradually became more talkative, and I developed a quiet friendship with Fatouma. Eventually they asked about my work, my personal life—about my mother, father, brother. They wondered about my wife. They worried that I had no children.

Out of respect I did not ask them personal questions. Even so, they slowly began to talk about their lives. Two of the younger women confessed to being between husbands and were hesitant to remarry, fearing another unstable marriage. They worried about their children who attended the local primary school. They were Zarma, Songhay-speaking people from east of the Niger River.

"Zarma are also strangers in Mehanna," Fatouma said, "so we know how hard it is to understand the people of the village."

During one of my visits, I offered to pound millet. The women laughed. "We don't think you would be good at pounding," Fatouma said. "It's women's work."

On one visit Fatouma asked me to remain after her friends returned to their homes. She offered me tea. We entered the shade of a thatch-covered veranda that fronted her mud brick thatch-roofed hut. She motioned for me to sit on a battered metal chair. Normally it would be unthinkable for a solitary woman to invite a male stranger to drink tea in her house. But Fatouma had no husband and was older than her friends, which in Songhay society gave her more social latitude.

Minutes later she brought out a familiar platter on which she had positioned a porcelain teapot, two small shot glasses, a large water glass, and a cone of sugar. She retreated inside her hut and brought out a brazier filled with glowing embers. She prepared tea in the same manner as did Adamu Jenitongo when he summoned me to sit and listen to important things. When she had completed the tea ritual, she thanked God for it and poured us both a glass. We let the tea cool a bit in the shot glasses and then began to sip.

Fatouma Seyni looked me up and down and stared directly into my eyes. "My life has been hard. I've been married three times— all bad. One husband beat me. One husband slept with other women and gave me the hot piss." She held out scarred forearms. "My last husband burned me with cigarettes." She looked at me with unblinking eyes. "In Niger women get divorced, and maybe get married again. Women between husbands often have to look after their children and take care of themselves." She paused. "I am no longer interested in men. If I do not marry again, I can live as I want to."

She put more tea and sugar into the pot and added water and then sat on the edge of her chair.

"I've heard about you. You're learning about *korte* [magic]. I know the people who are teaching you," she said. "Djibo and his father are my blood relatives. They say you are learning about spirits, the river, and witches."

I said that I was trying to learn all I could.

"I can see you have learned a lot, but they don't know everything. They can't teach you how to read the past, the present and the future."

"You mean *gounayan* [the art of looking]?" I asked eagerly. If she was a diviner, I said to myself, she would regularly receive both men and women in her home, which would also partially explain her willingness to drink tea with me.

"Yes. With the help of Nya Beri [the great mother spirit] and Dongo [deity of thunder] I can read shells."

"Are you willing to teach me?" I asked, cautiously enthusiastic about this possibility.

"You're not ready." she responded. "When you come back to Mehanna, we'll see if the spirits accept you. Come back and see me when you are ready."

As it turned out, five years passed before I saw Fatouma Seyni again. We did remain in contact. I wrote to her regularly and filled my letters to her with personal details and news of my life and my work. Like most rural women in Niger, my friend could neither read nor write, which meant she had to hire a student to read and translate my messages and write down her responses in French. In her messages she usually said that all was fine. She frequently thanked God for her continued good health. If I returned to Mehanna, she stated repeatedly, I should visit her.

During that time, I had returned to Niger on several occasions but spent most of my trip in Tillabéri with my mentor, Adamu Jenitongo, who was teaching me about the ways of the sorcerer. During that period, I often thought about Fatouma Seyni's invitation to learn how to see the past, present, and future. I wondered about when I might be ready. I had no idea what it meant to be ready or what I would do when the right time presented itself. I did know that if I wanted to learn divination I would have to wait until "my path opened," as Songhay elders liked to say. On one of my visits to Niger, Adamu Jenitongo performed a ritual to give me sight, the ability to read cowry shells. The results of the ritual did not appear to transform me.

"When will I be able to 'see'?"

"Your vision is like a baby's," my teacher said. "It must grow. In time you'll find your path."

When I received divinatory vision, I was a young American scholar who was weary of inscrutable statements like "you'll see," or "when the time is right," or "when your path opens." Nevertheless, I loved Niger and was determined to learn all I could. Each year, I would return for as long as I was able. Five years after I met Mehanna's female diviner, I returned to Niger to conduct more field research. After one week in Tillabéri, I went to Mehanna to visit old friends like Fatouma Seyni. From there I planned to take a motorized dugout upriver to the village of Ayoru, famous for its colorful market. From Ayoru, I hoped to cross the Niger and find a truck to Wanzerbe, the famous village of Songhay sorcerers.

In Mehanna market day is always a Thursday. I watched as people arrived on overburdened camels, horses, and donkeys. Niger River Island people came in overstuffed dugouts. Soon, the din of social renewal and price negotiation echoed in the dry hot air. Passing the leather smiths who offered beautifully stitched sandals and elaborate horse and camel saddles, I came upon a woman selling fried cakes—*massa,* in Songhay, made from either wheat, bean, or millet flour. I bought some bean cakes, my favorite, and saw my friend seated behind a display of dried okra, aromatic leaves, and squash. Although it had been five years since I had seen her, she looked exactly as she had on our morning visits in her village compound.

Seeing me, she smiled broadly.

I greeted her enthusiastically and inquired after her health.

"It has been a long time. They read your letters to me. Thank you."

"Many years." Out of respect I wanted to buy something from her. I asked about the price of squash. She mentioned a fair price. I paid her more.

She was pleased by my token generosity and beckoned me closer. "You've always shown me respect and listened to me. Maybe the time has come. This afternoon come to my compound and bring a vial of perfume to put in my *baata* [sacrificial container]."

When I arrived at her home, I presented her with Bint el Hadash, a special type of oil-based perfume. She frowned at it and said it might not be the right perfume, but we could try. I was impressed and excited about the possibility of taking lessons in divination. Adamu Jenitongo had talked to me about the baata, which is used to perform magic rites. Fatouma Seyni explained that her father had given her the power to read shells. "He saw it in the shells to teach me."

In the world of Songhay healing, male healers outnumber female practitioners. When female practitioners succeed, which is rare, their capacities often exceed those of their male counterparts.[3] Such was the case with my divination mentor. In our meetings over the years, she never talked about her considerable abilities, but when people in Mehanna learned about our friendship, they told me of her reputation as a powerful diviner. They said that she read shells for people in the village as well as for clients who traveled great distances to see her.

When we slipped inside her hut, she took out from under the bed her baata, a glass jar around which she had spun black thread. With some reluctance, she opened the lid and placed the vial of Bint al Hadash, among others, in the ritual container. She screwed the top back on and stood up.

"Let's go out and wait for an answer."

We returned to her veranda, sat down on palm frond mats, and chatted. Hearing of our visit, Fatouma Seyni's millet-pounding companions came by to greet us. They wondered if the market had been good. My friend, in fact, had earned enough money to buy some meat for the evening sauce. Looking at me, the women commented on my thin frame. When they left, Mehanna's powerful diviner stood up.

"We should go in to look in the baata."

Slowly, she unscrewed the container lid.

"You see," she said, "he didn't like that perfume!"

Inside the jar, the vial I had brought had been mysteriously smashed to bits. Incredibly, there was no trace of the Bint el Hadash scent.

"Go to the market and bring me Bint el Sudan."

I ran down the sandy path that led to the market and once again made my way to Abdou Kano's dry goods shop, a small rectangular structure stocked with bolts of cloth, sugar, tea, flashlights, batteries, mosquito nets, and many boxes of oil-based perfume.

"Do you have a girlfriend, Monsieur Paul?" Abdou asked. "How many vials of perfume are you going to buy today?"

Abdou was a short paunchy Hausa merchant from the east of Niger. He had three wives and almost a dozen children, and he laughed at the slightest provocation. Not answering his question, I paid for several vials of Bint el Sudan and made my way back to Fatouma's compound.

I gave her the "correct" perfume.

"Much better."

We reentered her house and repeated the same procedure. She carefully unscrewed the lid of her baata and placed one of the new vials inside. She then suggested we go outside once again and wait for a response. We sat down on her mats and waited.

"Does reading the shells bring you satisfaction?" I asked.

"It's a burden," she responded. "It's my obligation to help people with problems and pain. When my father gave me the power to see he warned me that I would pay a steep price for this special gift." She took a deep breath. "I have no children."

Clearly, she linked the sacrifice of children to the power to divine. Her admission stunned me. In a society in which people connected women's social standing to the presence of children, this loss was a great sacrifice indeed.

Mehanna's master diviner produced a pouch made of black cloth and opened it. She poured its contents—eleven cowrie shells—onto the sand. She cupped the shells in both her hands and recited an incantation. Then she spat four times on the shells, threw them onto the sandy ground, and observed the configurations.

"You see! He's accepted you. Can you smell it?"

The sweet scent of Bint el Sudan filled the air around us, a sign, according to Fatouma Seyni, that Dongo, deity of thunder, had accepted my offering. I took this as an indication that I was finally ready to learn how to read shells to uncover the past, understand the present, and predict the future. I felt overwhelmed and eager to begin. My mentor tempered my excitement.

Once again she said: "Reading shells is very serious. Sometimes you have to tell a person that something bad is going to happen."

"I understand," I said with some impatience. "Can I begin to learn to read the shells?"

"You are only ready to learn a little. When you come back to Mehanna, you can learn more. I've seen it in the shells."

As the shells predicted, I returned to Mehanna the next year to continue my studies. I had planned to visit Wanzerbe by way of Mehanna where I hoped to spend some time with Fatouma Seyni. On that trip, which took place during the peak of the hot season, the heat had been debilitating, which slowed to a sweaty crawl the pace of my studies. Even so, I left Tillabéri to travel to Mehanna. I had already learned a great deal from Adamu Jenitongo, but I still did not understand the predictive power of shells. I hoped to take up Fatouma Seyni's invitation. By the time I got to Mehanna by way of a bush taxi—a small, battered twelve-seat Toyota van—and a two-hour dugout trip poling upriver, I was exhausted. After customary greetings, my Mehanna friends showed me to my old compound. Eventually dinner arrived and we talked about our lives in the past year. Finally, I was able to sleep. The next day, toward late afternoon, I decided to visit Fatouma. I trudged through empty market space and made my way up the sandy path that led to compounds where Zarma people lived. As I walked uphill walled compounds gave way to millet-fenced living spaces. When I came upon Fatouma Seyni's compound, she saw me and clapped her hands. She recited the customary greetings.

"The letters said that you were coming soon. Thank God for your arrival."

"I thank God as well."

In the compound I noticed that my teacher had replaced her mud and straw hut with a two-room mud brick house.

"I had it built several months ago," she said.

I asked her about her health and the health of her kinspeople. She invited me into her new house. The thick walls and clean sand floors ensured a relatively cool temperature—even on a searing day in the Sahelian hot season. The front room featured a brightly painted armoire for her clothes and a crudely made sideboard for a set of porcelain plates, platters, and bowls. To one side of the sideboard she had stored two large cast iron cooking pots, the sides of which had turned black—from daily use on the hearth. At one end of the room, she had positioned a four-poster bed. Mosquito netting had been rolled up. On the straw mattress she had folded three colorful blankets, all of which had a checkerboard design—a typical Songhay pattern.

Fatouma Seyni unrolled two freshly made palm frond mats so we could sit down in the middle of her room. After a few moments, when we had talked and I had given her the gifts I brought for her, I asked if we could read the shells. In expectation of our session, I had brought the shells that Adamu Jenitongo had given me.

"Fatouma, shall we use your shells or mine?"

"Yours. I don't use mine anymore."

She said the spirit Dongo had told her to temporarily retire her shells. Perhaps she had seen too much sickness and death in them. I emptied twenty-one shells onto the sand in front of us. Just as in our past encounters, she picked up eleven shells, cupped them in her hands, recited an incantation, and then spit lightly on the shells.

I had hoped that her reading would bring news of excitement and adventure. Instead, she talked of people trying to block my path and my work. She saw health and happiness in my future and urged me to make regular offerings by placing perfumes and coins in my personal baata—all to protect family and friends. Like my previous experience with divination, these readings were somewhat disappointing. My teacher did describe with specificity the altar in my house and mentioned that she felt a good spirit had been shadowing me. She suggested that I give candy to the village children, money to the poor, and a white chicken and white goat to a blind man or woman. She assured me that if I performed these small acts the spirits would take care of me.

During the rest of my visit and future visits Fatouma Seyni offered me similar advice.

She taught me to distinguish females from males in shell configurations. I could read the presence of health, wealth, sickness, and death. I did not receive an answer to the fundamental issue in Songhay divination: How does the diviner determine the point of reference in the configuration of shells? Which shell, in the end, represents the client? My mentor in divination made it clear that I had to follow my own path into the light.[4]

Despite my limitations Fatouma Seyni's patient teachings enabled me to make slow progress on divination's path. I possessed cowrie shells that could *see*, shells that Adamu Jenitongo had buried in a termite hill for seven years. By the time he had harvested them, used them, and gave them to me, the cowries had the capacity to uncover the past, grasp the present, and envision the future. When I returned the United States, I kept the shells on an altar that I had put in the study of my home. They were a reminder of my time in Africa and my friendship with Fatouma Seyni.

As I began to throw shells, it was evident that inexperience restricted my capacity to read them. I could only make incomplete sense of the shell configurations. When I could fathom what the shells were *seeing*, the news would sometimes turn out to be something disturbing about loved ones, friends, or colleagues. If you read shells for someone, as Fatouma Seyni had warned me, you had to tell the unvarnished the truth—no matter how painful.

During my visits to Niger, I visited my friend as often as I could. Over the years, she had successes in several small trading ventures. As she aged, she enjoyed being a wise elder in the village. As guardians of cultural traditions, Songhay tend to treat older women, especially those who are healers or diviners, with considerable reverence.

Divination is much studied in anthropology. Scholars have tried to figure out how traces in the sand or the footprints of the pale fox among the Dogon of Mali translate into clairvoyance.[5] There are mathematical studies of divination that seek precise probabilistic answers to the mysteries of clairvoyance. There are studies that demonstrate the social and cultural dimensions of divinatory practice. There are even studies on the poetics of divination. These analyses are sophisticated attempts to understand divination. Even so, they do not explain—at least for me—the mystical aspects of the practice. How does the diviner know the point of reference in the configuration of the shells? What guides the diviner's interpretation of the shell configurations? Could diviners, as claimed by Adamu Jenitongo and Fatouma Seyni, hear the voices of spirits that guide their interpretation?[6]

Unlike Fatouma Seyni, I am no master of divination. My knowledge and interpretative skills are admittedly limited. To date, I've not yet fully understood how divination works. During my time in Mehanna I did learn that to understand divination, patience and the correct perfume are important. In exchange for whatever power or insight the special shells embodied, I learned that diviners are obligated to help others. Sometimes this aid exacts high personal cost. Having stepped, however gingerly, into the divinatory world, I developed respect for the courage and capacity of diviners. In retrospect I realized that my keen interest in sound and smell led me to Fatouma Seyni's doorstep, a vantage that provided me not only a glimpse into the complex lives of Songhay women but also an introduction into the tension-filled world of Songhay diviners. Working with their clients, these men and women routinely confront the vexing existential realities of what Hannah Arendt called the human condition—labor, work, action, love, hate, fidelity, betrayal, health, illness, life, and death—and do so with the grace that such momentous encounters require.[7]

I have not been to Niger in several years. Sadly, my more recent letters to Fatouma Seyni have not received responses. I wonder if she now lives with the ancestors. In my dreams about her, I am usually seated on a rusty metal chair in the shade of the jujube tree. We drink tea and talk. In my mind's eye, she is modest in style and character—and diligent. I am very grateful for the time she devoted to a stranger who did eventually leave the village but not without leaving behind a part of himself.

"I am part of a long tradition of women who through patience and suffering have learned to see and hear," she once said to me. "Like me, you must be serious about the world but not take yourself too seriously. And remember wisdom comes slowly and only comes to those who walk their path with patience and respect."

Fatouma Seyni's insights about the human condition have stayed with me. She taught me what she could and then sent me off to find my own way, which is, in the end, the Songhay way of acquiring knowledge. Given the passage of time and with patient persistence, we all learn to follow the path in our own way.

This chapter about the life and work of Fatouma Seyni is not simply a narrative about the presence and power of divination in African societies, however. For me it has broader implications. Fatouma Seyni's slow approach to learning runs counter to the "what have you done for me lately" ethos, as articulated in chapter 1, that has colonized academic life in the fast lane. In Fatouma Seyni's universe learning devolves from apprenticeship. Masters of knowledge take on apprentices, an act that creates a social and cultural bond between teachers and their apprentices. For Fatouma Seyni the acquisition of knowledge not only refined social relationships but was part of a lifelong process of maturation. As experience ripens your being, your mind develops, which means that at any point on the path of knowledge, you may not be ready to learn new elements of practice. Many apprentices, in fact, never gain complete mastery. Those who do become masters achieve it after many years of slow learning.[8]

Fatouma Seyni's prescription for acquiring divinatory skills also suggests a more embodied and sensuous approach to learning. To learn divination among the Songhay you need to sharpen your apprehension of the world. You need to learn how to look but also see, how to listen but also hear, how to touch but also feel. Put another way, divination requires that you reconfigure and refine your senses and open yourself to the world.

Ethnographic fieldwork has always required collaboration, but have those collaborations been the work of equals? My work with Fatouma Seyni and other Songhay elders has been an ongoing project that has embodied mutual respect, slow learning, and shared resources. As Jean Rouch once told me, the quality of an ethnography or an ethnographic film emerges from the quality of the long-standing relationships the ethnographer has developed in the field.

In the end, the winding path that I followed to Fatouma Seyni's compound exposed me to light in the shade of the jujube tree, a space on the periphery of things. In their recent collection, *Peripheral Methodologies: Unlearning, Not-knowing, and Ethnographic Limits*, Martínez, Di Puppo, and Frederiksen draw a map of the ethnographic periphery. In the book, the authors assume that invention emerges not from the center of things but from existential margins. In a context of unrivaled global complexity in which our tried-and-true explanations of social life no longer seem to work, what can social scientists do to confront the unanswerable, the ineffable—those things in human experience that defy comprehension? Indeed, Martínez, Di Puppo, and Frederiksen suggest that to move forward in our troubled times social scientists will have unlearn long-acknowledged methods and concepts, admit that they don't know, and accept ethnographic limits, all of which call for innovative ways of representing indigenous wisdom— "peripheral methodologies."[9]

In a very real sense, Fatouma Seyni spent her life on the periphery. She used the past to project into the future. Her divinatory practice extended beyond the threshold of verbal reasoning into a mysterious space where, as Nietzsche states, "logic bites its own tail." She taught me that incompleteness is acceptable and that it is perfectly fine to unlearn something that blocks a person's immersion in experience. Sometimes we must "unlearn" those things that compel us to close our being to the world. She always insisted on indirect teaching. She did not lecture me about shell configurations or how the mysterious divinatory spirit, Nya Beri, might one day whisper in my ear. For her, inexplicable phenomena did not create chaos or stress. She taught me that if you want to find the place where the sweet jujube tree is hidden, you must wander uneasily toward the periphery, the turbulent space of imagination and creativity.

Our sensuous journey along the periphery of things now takes us from the fragrant divinatory configurations in the dusty shade of Fatouma Seyni's jujube tree in Mehanna to the gripping sights, sonorous sounds, and pungent smells of a spirit possession ceremonies in Tillabéri. Through an evocation of the senses, I attempt to demonstrate how sensory description can flesh out the ethnography of religious phenomena, making them more accessible and meaningful to the public.

3

Sensory Dimensions of Spirit Possession

Che follo a si fonda hinka gana
"One foot cannot follow two paths."

Songhay proverb

More than four decades ago I witnessed my first Songhay spirit possession ritual. It took place in Tera, Niger, where I taught English as a foreign language at the secondary school. After a grueling series of afternoon lessons in devastatingly hot cement classrooms, my French colleagues and I repaired to the only bar in town, Chez Jacob, to enjoy a late afternoon beer. From our benches on the terrace of Jacob's one-room mud brick bar, we heard music—the *clack-roll-clacks* of gourd drums (*gasi*) and the *cries* of the monochord violin (*godji*). In the distance we saw a man dressed in a laboratory coat swirling about a rapidly expanding crowd. Even from a distance, we could see the man's eyes burned brightly. He groaned and spoke in pidgin French.

An old man approached me, the only teacher there who understood some of the Songhay language.

"The doctor," he said, pointing to the man in the laboratory coat, "wants to meet you."

Looking at what seemed, to my untrained eye, a hideous figure, I said, "Well, I don't want to meet him."

"You must," the old man said. "If you don't see him, it will be bad times for our village." He raised his arms toward the sky. "Please?"

With great hesitation, I approached the man in the laboratory coat. In his left hand, he held a syringe that contained a milky fluid. Seeing me, the man-spirit spoke.

"Enchanted to meet you," he said.

"Enchanted," I said.

"Your mother has no tits."

"Yes, she does," I insisted, which provoked great laughter.

"Your father has no balls."

"He does," I said. "He does."

More laughter.

The man-spirit held out his hand for me to shake. When I did so, I felt an inexplicable electric shock, which jolted me into a different universe of meaning, a place where spirits in the bodies of mediums mingle with human beings, sometimes inspiring them, sometimes terrifying them.

Given its centrality to Jean Rouch's work, spirit possession was sometimes a topic of conversation at the sessions I attended in Rouch's Musée de l'Homme projection room (see introduction). On one occasion Rouch talked at length about his long association with Songhay spirits and spirit practitioners in the Republic of Niger. He described his first encounter with Kalia, a spirit priestess and grandmother of Damouré Zika, who in the 1940s had been the foreman of Rouch's roadbuilding crew of laborers. Rouch explained that during some roadbuilding in the dry, vast, and desiccated scrub bush west of the Niger River, lightning had struck and killed one of the crew members. Frightened by this turn of events, no one wanted to continue to work on what they considered to be sacred land. Damouré Zika suggested that his grandmother, Kalia, could fix the situation. A day later Kalia arrived.

FIGURE 5
Hauka spirit possession, Tillabéri, Niger. © Paul Stoller.

She was a short, slight woman who that day wore an indigo-dyed homespun tunic over a wraparound skirt of the same fabric and color. Kalia said that the Thunder God's land had been desecrated. Dongo, she explained, used lightning to strike those who dared violate his domain. At a crossroads in the bush near the village of

Gangel, a place where the spirit and social worlds intersect, a musician played Dongo melodies on a one-string violin. Kalia walked up to the laborer's enshrouded corpse and spit fresh milk onto it—to purify the body. Moving onto the crossroads, she sprinkled the sacred space with Bint el Sudan, the sweet-smelling oil-based perfume linked to Dongo (see chapter 2). The pungent scent of Bint el Sudan soon permeated the air. The cries of the one-string violin echoed in the dry air. When a praise singer recited the old words, the sounds of which attract spirits to their mediums, Hauka (spirits of colonialization associated with Dongo) violently invaded the bodies of several laborers. Saliva frothed from their mouths. They handled fire. They ate poisonous plants. They praised their master, Dongo. In time, they asked people for contributions. Having witnessed Songhay spirit possession for the first time, Rouch said that it was operatic—beautiful, artful, and profound. From that moment on, spirit possession became the centerpiece of Rouch's writings and his films.[1]

The observation and analysis of spirit possession, an embodied performance par excellence, is a window into how the senses can—and should—be represented in artful ethnographic description. Spirit possession underscores the drama of life in the world. In its various articulations, spirit possession's sensuously embodied symbolism highlights existential relations of earth and sky, village and bush, past and present, men and women, old and young, well-being and suffering, health and illness, and life and death.

In this way spirit possession articulates powerfully the drama of the human condition. As Roger Bastide long ago suggested, it is a dramatic religious experience during which human beings come face to face with the supernatural, during which people interact with deities. For these reasons, Bastide suggested, spirit possession has a long history in the ethnographic record.[2] In the nineteenth century anthropologists considered spirit possession as either an expression of primitive mentality or an aberrant state of being.[3] Scholars extended the aberrant behavior framework into studies of possession as "hysteria," which persisted well into twentieth- century anthropology.[4] Because of its drama and its existential centrality to issues that underscore social life, scholars have long tried to explain the phenomenon of spirit possession—with limited success.

The anthropological record on spirit possession has great depth and breadth, but do ethnographies of spirit possession adequately capture the sensorial dimensions of these dramatic ritual performances? What do we miss when we excise the senses from our descriptions and analyses? In this chapter, I suggest that the anthropology of spirit possession tends to be sensorially inadequate. The artful inclusion of the sensorial description of any performance enriches immeasurably the anthropological record as well as our comprehension of the existential parameters of the human condition—especially in troubled times.

Anthropologists have a long history of theorizing spirit possession. In this record of scholarship scholars have framed their analyses through a set of paradigms, the explanatory power and applicability of which has waxed and waned over the years. No matter the paradigm, though, most writers have backgrounded the sensory dimension of spirit possession performances. In my view, there have been five major forms of explanation that anthropologists have used in their attempt to explain spirit possession—functionalist (sociological), psychoanalytic (psychological), physiological (biological), symbolic (cultural), and theatrical (performance).

Functionalism has a long history in anthropology. Originally following a line of thought they borrowed from the biological study of ecosystems, functionalists and structural functionalists sought to understand how groups might maintains social equilibrium through time. Their premise was—and is—that as people in social groups pursue their interests, social life becomes fraught with conflict. Social tensions arise between men and women, old and young, blood relative and affine, and village person and stranger. Given the variety of conflicting tensions in society, functionalists pinpoint how social groups manage to resolve conflicts—at least for a short period of time. In various guises functionalism shaped the description and analysis of mid-twentieth-century anthropologists, particularly those of the British persuasion. I certainly don't want to commit too much space to a review of a vast and, from today's perspective, rather uninteresting literature. Suffice it to suggest that in their attempt to explain spirit possession, functionalists considered it a mechanism that would ease the burdens of social conflict and restore social harmony. Considering that tension between men and women has long been a centerpiece of social relations, functionalists would argue that the preponderance of female spirit mediums in the global array of spirit possession groups means that spirit possession is a very good way to diffuse the social stressors brought on through gender inequities. Somehow, or so the argument goes, the powerful experience of spirit mediumship in which women suddenly get to be formidable personages during a ritual enables spirit mediums to adapt to the strictures of gender discrimination in everyday life. In this way mediums enjoy fleeting moments of prestige. The power of this kind of analysis is that it demonstrates how spirit possession is a dynamic social process with concrete social consequences. Even so, functionalist analyses of spirit possession, in which scholars focus preeminently on the sociology of mediumship, generally overlook the cultural condition of women in society and bypass the embodied, sensuous aspects of mediumship and ritual processes.[5]

Much of the scholarship on spirit possession has considered the psychology of individual mediums. What is it about the play of psychological forces that makes a particular person a good candidate for spirit mediumship? In the psychoanalytic version of spirit possession analysis, which has been a major orientation among French anthropologists, the medium, to put it simply, experiences a culturally specific psychotic event and seeks the counsel of a spirit priest. The spirit priest diagnoses the spirit sickness, or pre-possession malady, and recommends a set of ritualized therapeutics that culminate in an initiation ceremony in which mediums are welcomed to the community. Thereafter, the psychotic behaviors disappear, and mediums serve important roles in their communities. Indeed, they lend their bodies to the world. For French anthropologists of the psychoanalytic persuasion, this practice conforms to the model of (a) social disintegration (psychotic behaviors), (b) catharsis (initiation), and (c) reintegration (mediumship). As in the functionalist model of spirit possession, this orientation does not consider adequately the cultural, embodied, and/or phenomenological dimensions of spirit possession. In addition, scholars in this tradition usually background the social consequences of spirit possession, which, lest we forget, functionalists analyze with methodological precision.[6]

Studies of spirit possession have not escaped from the long social science tradition of reducing complex social and cultural phenomena to biological processes. These studies consider the physiology of possession states. What happens to the medium's body when she or he experiences trance? Do dietary restrictions create the right mix of physiological elements that might induce an altered state of consciousness—a possessed state? Scholars have strapped electrodes to entranced spirit mediums to measure how the state of possession alters brainwaves. Other scholars have studied how the rhythmic drumming alters brainwave activity such that it induces trance. Still others have considered how swinging and twirling, two activities often associated with spirit possession ceremonies, disturb the inner ear in a way that brings the onset of an altered state. There are also more purely biologically reductive works, mostly cross-cultural in nature, that link possession to deficiencies in diet.[7] These studies tend to minimize the social and cultural aspects of spirit possession and reduce the phenomenon to a set of biological determinants. This kind of analysis misses most of the social, cultural, and psychological elements that are embodied in spirit possession. Scholars of this theoretical bent also fail to consider the sensuously contoured elements of performance that render spirit possession symbolically powerful and culturally meaningful.

From the late nineteenth century to well into the twentieth, anthropologists who studied spirit possession paid scant attention to what spirits—in the bodies of their mediums—actually said to people who attended ceremonies. George Balandier, a French sociologist, was one of the first scholars to take a more culturally symbolic approach to spirit possession, considering it a form of intellectual communication. Taking a similar tack, Michael Lambek and Janice Boddy wrote ethnographies of spirit possession in which they focused attention on the nuanced symbolism of the ceremonies.[8] Tuning in to interpretative frequencies of Paul Ricoeur and Clifford Geertz, scholars began to consider spirit possession as a *text* that communicated messages of cultural significance—the previously mentioned relations of earth to heaven, bush to village, men to women, illness to health, and life to death. As I once suggested:

> The strength of such a theoretical model is that it explores the complexities of local expression and local ideas. The weakness of

this kind of analysis, however, is that in considering the cultural content, analysts sometimes neglect the social and psychological aspects. Some writers who employ this analytic model, moreover, over-emphasize possession's textuality, relying too much upon the assumption that images and other sensations (sound, smell, taste) are "texts." Generally, not even the best of these symbolic studies, which combine the symbolic, psychological and/social aspects of the phenomenon, present holistic accounts of spirit possession. An exception is Roger Bastide's monumental *The African Religions of Brazil* (1978), which was based upon the author's slowly developed participation in *Candomblé*, the major spirit possession practice in Brazil. And yet even Bastide's intimate perspective seems to under-emphasize spirit possession as an embodied cultural practice.[9]

Put another way, even the best cultural analyses of spirit possession tend to neglect how the senses impact spirit possession performances.

Spirit possession, then, is a dramatic event during which human beings physically and psychologically confront supernatural beings in the bodies of mediums, which makes it a cultural performance. French scholars like André Schaeffner, Michel Leiris, Gilbert Rouget, and Jean-Marie Gibbal long ago suggested that spirit possession was a form of cultural theater.[10] Using this theatrical framework, spirit priests become directors, mediums are actors, the dance ground is a stage, and spirit speech is converted into texts that underscore those existential issues germane to a group's cosmology and cosmogony. In my own work on spirit possession, *Fusion of the Worlds*, I was much taken with the theatrical explanation of it, but in the end I admitted that the model could take one's comprehension only so far—a stage for an incomplete and ofttimes Eurocentric analysis of non-Western cultural phenomena.[11]

At the conclusion of *Fusion of the Worlds*, I suggested that a more embodied and sensuous representation of spirit possession would showcase the importance of the sentient body and demonstrate a powerful relationship among bodily practices (in this case spirit possession), cultural memory, and political power.[12] This approach constitutes a more phenomenological orientation to social and cultural description, which, in turn, owes a great debt to the development of sensorial anthropology. Responding to the dominance of sensuous body-as-text metaphors in the social science literature, I wrote:

> In anthropology it is especially important to consider... smells, tastes, textures, and sensations, particularly in those societies in which the Eurocentric notion of text—and textual interpretations—are not important—I have noted elsewhere why it is representationally and analytically important to consider how perception in non-Western societies devolves not simply from vision (and the linked metaphors of reading and writing) but also from smell, taste, touch and hearing. In many of these societies these "lower" senses are central to the metaphoric organization of experience; they also trigger cultural memory.[13]

In the late twentieth century most anthropologists, including, of course, scholars of spirit possession, developed their theories in the absence of sensory studies. How might a scholar evoke the importance of smell, sound, taste, and smell in her or his anthropological work? It is almost impossible for people in the more visually oriented societies in Europe and North America to contemplate such a refined sensorial analysis. In Europe and North America most people *see* the truth and *envision* reality. It is hard to imagine how to smell, touch, or taste truth or reality. Even so, a group of anthropologists have attempted—with no small amount of success—to incorporate elements of the sensorium into anthropological descriptions of social worlds.

Such a tack has been felicitous. When people confront the world in which they live, they use all the senses. Aside from the pioneering work of Walter Ong, whose *The Presence of the Word* (1967) would set the foundation for a future study of the so-called lower senses, most social science scholars have tended to spatialize—a practice of visualization—the nonvisual senses.[14] In so doing they have adhered themselves to the bloodless prose of plain style, which has long been the foundation of (social) scientific discourse. Guided by Ong's contribution as well as the provocative work of Victor Zuckerkandl on the philosophical dimensions of sound in the world, Steven Feld published the first sensorially contoured anthropological work, *Sound and Sentiment*, an ethnography about the existential importance of sound in a densely forested highland New Guinea environment in which vision is limited. Other anthropological works on sound followed.[15]

In time, image-conscious anthropologists refined their approach to vision and set the parameters for visual anthropology, which had focused almost entirely on the production and analysis of ethnographic film. Several visual anthropologists, however, took a more phenomenological multisensorial approach to the visual and put forward thoughtful books and essays about how human beings see the world.[16]

As this early work progressed, a group of anthropologists at Concordia University began to compare all the senses across a wide variety of societies. David Howes, an important scholar of sensorial anthropology and the director of the Concordia Sensoria Research Group, became interested in sensorial ratios. Why might vision, sound, smell, or taste be more primary in a group's sensorial organization of experience? That work launched a more sustained analysis of sensoria around the world.

To date, there have been two approaches to the anthropological analysis of the sensorium: a theory-building analytical orientation to the senses and a more descriptively ethnographic representation of sensoria. There is no shortage of analytical works on vision, smell, sound, touch, and taste. Many of these texts focus on the attempt to isolate sensorial principles of universal application.[17] During these developments other scholars, including several anthropologists, have considered the science of sensation—the chemistry of taste and smell, the phenomenology of sound, and the sensorial dimensions of visual culture.[18] These works have enhanced our comprehension of the human sensorium.

A second group of scholars have taken a more broadly phenomenological approach to the representation of sensoria. They have attempted to use ethnographic description to evoke the senses in prose, art installations, and film. Anthropologists like Ruth Behar, Michael Taussig, Michael Jackson, Robert Desjarlais, Piers Vitebsky, and Kirin Narayan have used sensuous prose to evoke the sensory dimensions of people and the places in which they live.[19]

Like these ethnographically orientated authors, I too believe that form and style can provide powerfully evocative representations of sensory worlds. In my own ethnographic work, which has foregrounded narrative, I have attempted to evoke the distinctive sounds, smells, texture, vistas, and tastes of social life in West Africa and among West Africans in New York City.[20] In the attempt to give the reader a sensory feel of a place, I have tried to weave these sensuous descriptions of social life into the fabric of my texts, including works on spirit possession among the Songhay people of Niger.

As I suggested in the introduction, one of the cardinal rules of writing evocative nonfiction, including, of course, ethnographic nonfiction, is to *show* as well as *tell*. In most academic writing, including most anthropological writing, scholars have been taught to *tell*, not *show*, which means that most scholars devote most of their texts to explication and analysis. Instead of using techniques that vividly show us the workings of social processes, we lapse into prosaic prose to explain sorcery, kinship, exchange, and spirit possession. There is nothing wrong with explication, but as a textual tack *telling* tends to produce long, jargon-filled texts that often obscure what the writer is trying to describe and/or explain. As I've been suggesting in these pages, ethnographic texts that *show* as well as *tell* are more likely to be read and reread.

How does one write something that evokes a theme? There are two ways to evoke social phenomena and social performance: narrative and the vivid description of sensoria. These two tacks are far from being mutually exclusive. Fiction writers have long used sensory evocation to spice up their texts and bring life and drama to the stories they are attempting to recount.

My work *Fusion of the Worlds*, for example, was a textual experiment. For me, the sensuous power and symbolic depth of Songhay spirit possession had been so sensorially overwhelming that I long struggled to find a way to describe its fast sweep of action, let alone come to some fundamental understanding of its ritual elaborations. After many false starts, I decided to try to let sensuous descriptions carry the analytical burden of the text. Following the powerful insights articulated in Edward Said's *Beginnings*, I wanted to *show* my experimental intentions at the very outset of the text, which would, or so I hoped, set a textual foundation for the book.[21] Here's how I attempted to sensuously set the scene for my ethnography of Songhay spirit possession, *Fusion of the Worlds*:

Clack! A sharp sound shattered the hot, dry air above Tillaberi. Another clack, followed by a roll and another *clack-roll-clack*, pulsed through the stagnant air. The sounds seemed to burst from the dune that overlooked the secondary school of the town of a thousand people, mostly Songhay-speaking, in the Republic of Niger.

The echoing staccato broke the sweaty boredom of a hot afternoon in the hottest town in one of the hottest countries in the world and, like a large hand, guided hearers up the dune to Adamu Jenitongo's compound to witness a possession ceremony.

The compound's three-foot millet stalk fence enclosed Adamu Jenitongo's dwellings: four straw huts that looked like beehives. At the compound's threshold, the high-pitched whine of the monochord violin greeted me. Inside, I saw the three drummers seated under a canopy behind gourd drums. Although the canopy shielded them from the blistering Niger sun, sweat streamed down their faces. Their sleeveless tunics clung to their bodies; patches of salt had dried white on the surface of their black cotton garments. They continued their rolling beat. Seated behind them on a stool was the violinist, dressed in a red shirt that covered his knees. Despite the intensity of the heat and the noise of the crowd, his face remained expressionless as he made his instrument *cry*.[22]

Sound is a principal sense in Songhay spirit possession ceremonies. Sound connects past and present, heaven and earth. It connects the spirit and social worlds. The sound of the godji, or monochord violin, is sacred. This special instrument is fashioned from a gourd that is covered with a special lizard skin (called *bo* in Songhay) and strung with hair from the tail of a *sobe* horse, which is a black stallion with a white patch face. Musicians play the instrument with a bow fashioned from a curved piece of wood or curved metal and strung with the same horsehair. When played the violin produces a high-pitched whine. Songhay elders say that the godji cries (*a ga heh*) for the past, the present, and the future;

FIGURE 6
Sound in Songhay spirit possession. © Paul Stoller.

it cries for the harmony in the world. These cries lure the spirits, which live in the first of seven heavens, to the bodies of their mediums.[23]

One would think that the profound and symbolically powerful cries of the godji would be sufficient to bring the onset of spirit possession. They are not. These sounds must be combined with the clack-roll-clacks of the gourd drums. The mix of cries and rhythmic clack-roll-clacks compel dancers, usually older women who are spirit mediums, to move onto the dance ground. As the sounds enter their bodies, their movements pulse with energy. They sway to the melodic tempo, moving counterclockwise. When the tempo quickens, they form a straight line. In sync with the sound, they stomp their feet and, like birds flapping their wings, move their arms up and down as their old faces crease into ecstatic smiles. This mix of sound and movement, however, is not always sufficient to bring on possession. As the mediums continue to dance, the *sorko*, praise singer to the spirits, begins to recite the old words:

> She gave birth to suntunga. She gave birth to mantunga. The sah tree, the dugu tree . . . wali belinga, kasa tobe. Dikko is the owner of the big festival. Dikko is the owner of the small festival. The mother of all peasants. The father of all peasants. You must protect us all.

The sound of the old words often brings tears to the eyes of mediums. Hearing them, the mediums begin to shake. They stammer, bellow, and groan. External entities enter their bodies, transforming them from human being to spirit. As the sorko continues to recite the old words, attendants give the spirits their costumes—a particular hat, a satin sash, a hatchet encased in red leather with a small bell attached to its head.

One of my Songhay teachers, a sorko named Kada Mounmouni, explained the power of sound. The music, he suggested, enters the bodies of dancers. As for the old words, Kada Mounmouni told me that their power lies less in what the words mean than in the sounds they project, which, in the end, complete the sound sequences that enable the onset of spirit possession.

But the Songhay spirits are very demanding. The cries of the godji, the clack-roll-clacks of the gourd drums, and the sonorous contours of the old words do not necessarily ease the passage of a spirit into the body of its medium. Songhay practitioners also use the sweet scent of oil-based perfumes to facilitate the fusion of the spirit and social worlds. As noted in chapter 2, perfumes are associated with a spirit or a particular family of spirits. There are five such families in the Songhay pantheon. When the sorko senses that the spirit is near, he takes out the appropriate vial of perfume and douses the dancer with drops of fragrance, the sensuous power of which intoxicates the air. These smells have an electric effect as if the dancer's body has been jolted with supernatural energy. The sorko continues to empty his perfume vial, which compels the spirit to speak to the audience.

The sense of touch also plays a significant role in understanding the otherworldliness of Songhay spirit possession. In the narrative that opens this chapter, a Hauka handshake electroshocked me into an unimaginable dimension of spiritual reality. The Hauka spirit's touch upended my avowedly Western sensibilities, creating a situation in which nothing made sense, a moment in which logic, returning once again to Nietzsche's *Birth of Tragedy*, bites its own tail.

Touch in Songhay spirit possession is also a matter of connecting to the earth from which grows life-sustaining millet and sorghum. When the *genji bi,* which in Songhay means "black spirits," take the bodies of their mediums, the latter bare their chests and pick up handfuls of soil to shower their bodies. In this way these earth spirits, which have ancestral links to the land they first inhabited, demonstrate their primordial power to ensure soil fertility.

Spirits use the sense of touch in other ways. Consider the Hauka, the spirits of various colonial identities that are featured in Jean Rouch's unforgettable film, *Les maîtres fous.* When they come into the bodies of their mediums, the mediums touch burning torches and put their hands into cauldrons of boiling stew—with no ill effects.[24] In the same vein, consider the *Doguwa* spirits, which represent historic cultural clashes that merged from the late nineteenth-century migration of Hausa-speaking peoples from eastern to western Niger. These spirits like to rub hot ash on people they like.

Taste also plays a role in Songhay spirit possession, though the presence of this sense is a bit more limited than that of smell, touch, or sound. To demonstrate their otherworldliness, spirits taste and consume forbidden foods—untransformed bushmeat like dogs, bush rodents, and wild game—the taste of which is supposedly unpalatable. In some cases, Songhay cut the throats of this kind of game, which transforms its taste and palatability from bush to village meat. In the bodies of their mediums, however, spirits do not transform what is offered to them, which is a social transgression that demonstrates their supernatural otherness. Spirits in the bodies of their mediums may also consume sour and bitter plants, some of which provoke severe vomiting, some of which are toxic. In addition, spirits are offered "thick" foods, stews that are laced with butter oil and the sweet juice of hippo grass (*burgu*) or millet porridge mixed with sweet cream and butter oil. These foods and the tastes (sweet, sour, bitter) associated with them honor the presence of spirits on earth.

Visual imagery is essential in Songhay spirit possession. As evident from a perusal of Jean Rouch's films, these events are filled with vivid images: colorful costumes such as Dongo's homespun indigo-dyed cape or the black-and-white striped tunics worn by the earth spirits, or the pith helmets, swagger sticks, and fan belt whips that Hauka display. The spirits also carry ritual objects. Dongo likes to wield his red leather encased hatchet. Cirey, spirit of lightning, carries a staff wrapped in black or red leather. Sometimes the earth spirits dance with an antelope horn, also encased in red leather.

During ceremonies, image mixes with movement. As previously mentioned, spirit mediums move counterclockwise (*windi*) on the dance ground, producing an image of a moving circle, which designates a sacred space within. When the tempo quickens, mediums begin the *gani*, a foot-stomping, arm-flapping dance in sacred space. As they move toward sacred sounds and old words, they invite the onset of possession.

From this brief description of the sensory elements of Songhay spirit possession it is clear that in ritual performances or, for that matter, in the performance of everyday life, the presence of the senses is profound. Sensory displays of sound, taste, touch, vision, and smell are usually not isolated from one another; rather, as

Figure 7
The flow of spirit possession, Djamona, Niger. © Paul Stoller.

events unfold, they blend dynamically. Indeed, an apprehension of the senses in social life tends to be synesthetic. Writing about the experience of gustation, Barbara Kirshenblatt-Gimblett stressed how synesthesia is central to the human experience of taste. "From color, steam rising, gloss and texture, we infer taste, smell and feel. Taste is something we anticipate and infer from how things look, feel to the hand, smell (outside the mouth), and sound. Our eyes let us 'taste' food at a distance by activating the sense memories of taste and smell."[25]

In the same manner listening to someone is more than engaging in sound exchanges. Consider the notion of *deep listening*.

> When we listen to people telling us a story, which is a performance, do we hear them? Does listening to stories enable us to connect to other people—to hear them? How can we develop the skills to hear our loved ones, our friends, our colleagues and especially people who are different? How do men hear women? How do women hear men? How can black folks and white folks hear one another? Can people of diverse ethnicity listen to and hear one another?[26]

In the contemporary era, these are sometimes the questions that have war-and-peace, life-and-death consequences. The South African anthropologist Rosabelle Boswell has long considered the sensuous dimensions of deep listening. In a brilliant essay Boswell wrote that the

> narrative imperative is also a sensuous imperative; that is, while story-telling is (obviously) a form of "verbal communication," it just as fundamentally involves "nonverbal communication" (e.g. looks, gestures, smells). In practice, listening to a story entails attending to the "interconnection" of the senses, no less than experiencing the "interconnections" between storyteller and audience (Finnegan 2014). Put another way, story-telling is at once a social activity and "sense-making activity" (Vannini et al. 2012), which

> calls for sense-work. . . . Stories are (potentially) addressed to all the
> senses, even taste (e.g. savouring the "sweetness" of a tale), not just
> the ears, particularly in the context of face-to-face story-telling.[27]

Indeed, "one might observe the storyteller 'settling in' to relate his story, become more animated in conveying his account, sustaining eye contact, eyes tearing up, touching or gripping the listener to make a point. Attending to the sensuality of storytelling/listening deepens the listener's analytical capabilities enabling him or her access to the non-aural dimensions of stories."[28]

Boswell goes on to show how the sensuous give-and-take of storytelling and deep listening triggers the texture of the past, the bitterness of oppression, and the sourness of dispossession, especially in contexts of social inequality that have developed between north and south, between the colonizer and the colonized, and between men and women. These divides create spaces that make it easy for us to misunderstand and be misunderstood, to silence and be silenced. They can isolate us in hermetically sealed universes of meaning. In depicting her highly nuanced encounters with Indian Ocean Island peoples, Boswell describes the evolution of her own practice of deep listening. "Thus, as I did, they may eat to taste the past, reinstate a stance of authority in order to maintain dignity in the story-listening process, recoil to eschew public vulnerability and allow themselves to feel euphoria. Listening to hear may also assist anthropologists to publicly and unashamedly come to terms with the profoundly political aspects of fieldwork."[29]

In the end what can one say about the anthropology of senses? It does analyze the history and aestheticization of sensoria as well as the relation of the senses to social identity and to social change. It also considers the sensuous dynamics of sensoria and how they relate to phenomena like synesthesia. Writing about the sense of taste in anthropology and by extension the other senses in social life, David Sutton concluded:

> The deployment of recent, intertwining approaches from the anthropology of the senses, phenomenology, materiality studies, and theories of value, among others, provides exciting opportunities for rich ethnographic elaboration. And the focus on sensory aspects experienced like few other things both inside and outside of bodies (and transformed in the crossing of bodily boundaries) means that these approaches have much to gain from an engagement with food. But our theoretical progress has yet to be matched by any corpus of rich ethnographies that make the sensory aspects of food central to an understanding of lives and experiences; many of the writings on this topic remain in the form of short, suggestive articles or snippets of ethnography in larger works on other topics.[30]

When it comes to the evocation of the senses in the social description of the performance of ritual or of everyday life, there is much more to do to chart a course to a strong future of ethnographic writing and anthropology.

Like David Sutton, I believe that anthropologists have just begun to savor fully the senses of social worlds. To produce sensuous ethnographies that meet the challenges of our times, perhaps we need to emulate Jean Rouch and Lisbet Holtedahl and slow down in a fast world full of expectations and distractions. It takes time to develop the kind of deliberate sensibility underscored in the slow food movement, which I mentioned briefly in chapter 1. In 1989 Carlo Petrini, an Italian activist and journalist, formally set up an international slow food organization in Paris. From its very beginning, the slow food movement was less a platform for recipes of sumptuous slow cooking than a sustained cultural critique of life in the fast lane of contemporary society. Beyond its critique of the endless array of tasteless offerings in fast food restaurants, the slow movement disparages the widespread anonymity of so-called Facebook friendships, the dearth of face-to-face conversations, and the global corporatization of social relations.[31]

Enter the anthropology of the senses. As the work of sensorial anthropologists has demonstrated, it takes many years to develop the ethnographic sensitivities to understand the significant symbolic, social, and political dynamics of sensory worlds. It is through a slowly developed anthropology that one can understand how the senses can bring shape and definition to ritual or to everyday performances.

During the first years of my field research among the Songhay people in the Republic of Niger, a healer taught me an important lesson. We had been treating a man suffering from what seemed to me a deadly illness. The healer said that the man's soul had been stolen from his body and that if we didn't find it and liberate it, the patient would die. I accompanied him to the outskirts of the village. When we came upon mounds of discarded millet husks, he sifted through the debris to find the sick man's soul. Suddenly, he jumped up and proclaimed that the sick man's soul had been liberated. He asked me if I had noticed the man's soul.

I shrugged my shoulders.

He looked at me, shook his head and said: "You look but you don't see. You touch but you do not feel. You listen but you don't hear. It will take many years for you to learn how to see, feel, and hear the world."[32]

Will we take the time to develop the sensory capacity to sense the worlds we attempt to describe and represent ethnographically? Songhay teachers liked to tell me that although a path may be long, it is well worth taking, especially if it enables you to explore the delicacies of taste in social life. In the next chapter I consider how taste can destroy and/or reestablish social harmony.

4

Tasting Harmony in the World

Haam'issa fumbu ga doonu hassara
"[A piece of] rotten fish will spoil millet porridge"
Songhay proverb

I first heard the rotten fish proverb decades ago at the end of a rather rotten meal that I had shared in Adamu Jenitongo's compound. After a two-year hiatus I was back to conduct more anthropological fieldwork in Tillabéri, Niger. As always, my teacher and his family—a sister, two wives, two sons, a motley crew of cousins, and many scantily clad grandchildren—welcomed the white man who speaks Songhay into their home. Among Songhay people, a stranger is treated like a god in your house. In an uncomfortably poor land, the sages say that the stranger should be given the best accommodations and fed with sumptuous meals replete with meat, chicken, and copious amounts of sauce laced with butter oil. If these sauces also feature the sweet juice of the *burgu* plant, a grass that grows in the shallows of the Niger River, family pride is reinforced. Songhay elders like to say that treating the stranger with generosity and respect brings harmony and balance to the world.

With that set of expectations, the rancidly sour taste of rotten sauce, which was served on the second-to-last night of the visit, created a moment of disharmony and imbalance, which compelled my teacher to recite the rotten fish proverb. What set of conditions created the context for the preparation and presentation of rotten sauce?

The next morning Tillabéri's powerful healer admitted the obvious: social life had grown tense in his Tillabéri compound. A young woman from another ethnic group, the Fulani, had married his youngest son. During that stint of fieldwork no one seemed particularly pleased with Djenaba, whose appearance—tall, thin, with an aquiline nose and copper-colored skin—underscored her social and cultural difference. As the youngest in-law in the compound, people expected her to do the lion's share of the household work—fetching water, cleaning pots and pans, sweeping the compound of debris, trekking into town to buy condiments, not to mention cooking lunch and dinner. Djenaba performed these incessant chores with quiet dignity. During that period hardly anyone expressed appreciation for her efforts. What's more, people in the compound did not often call her by her name. Instead, they called her *debbo*, which in the Fulani language means "woman." Indeed, during my time there I rarely saw her smile or laugh.

What might a young Fulani woman in a Songhay compound do to improve her social situation? In a society in which women, especially women who are *other*, can exercise few, if any, rights, how might Djenaba express the poignancy of her alienation? She could divorce her husband and return to her family—a shameful act the emotional costs of which would far outweigh the social benefits. She could verbally object to her treatment, but given her marital status and her gender, such protest would fall on deaf ears and probably deepen her alienation.

When guests arrived in the compound, Djenaba may well have understood that a perfect storm of social factors had formed on the horizon. When that storm moved through the compound, she might be able to express herself in a forceful manner. Consider these factors. As the most junior spouse in the compound, Adamu Jenitongo's wives asked her to prepare special meals for honored guests. As previously mentioned, these meals should be of the highest quality—good cuts of beef, sumptuously thick sauces filled with aromatic spices and laced with butter oil. These are known as *thick sauces*, which should be served in *thick* situations like feeding an honored guest. During that one-month sojourn, which would be considered a thick situation, Djenaba, who was not passionate about cooking, produced thick sauces that were acceptable, but hardly sumptuous. What would happen if, at the right moment, she delivered a profoundly *thin* sauce? Would people in the compound feel a degree of empathy for the sourness of her alienation?

The second-to-last night of the visit, Djenaba decided to prepare *fukko hoy*, a thin sauce lacking meat, made from the dried leaves of the *fukko* plant, which, if prepared correctly, produces a slightly sour taste that Songhay people covet. If the fukko sauce is not prepared correctly, it turns so rancidly sour that it is impossible to eat. Knowing these culinary particulars, Djenaba produced a profoundly thin sauce the sourness of which brought shame to Adam Jenitongo's Tillabéri compound and provoked the recitation of the rotten fish proverb.

The rotten sauce scene disrupted social life in my teacher's home. A dust cloud of shame settled over the compound. Djenaba had expressed her discomfort and displeasure. In a moment of social defiance, she had disrupted social harmony. Through the powerful sense of taste, she had attracted the attention of all her in-laws who the next day didn't miss an opportunity to insult her insolence and castigate her ethnicity.[1]

What can we take away from the gustatory experience of rotten sauce in a remote compound in West Africa? The ethnographic richness of this minor incident demonstrates powerfully how taste is much more than a culinary exercise. Indeed, the sensuous experience of taste can shape our social relations and configure the emotional contours of our well-being, which, as I'll attempt to suggest in this chapter, is a central theme in the anthropological approach to taste-in-the-world.

There are many challenges to confront when one sets out to explore taste in the world. It is almost impossible for people in the more visually oriented societies in Europe and North America to contemplate such a refined gustatory analysis. In Europe and North America most people *see* the truth and *envision* reality. It is hard to imagine how to smell, feel, or taste truth or reality.

As I suggested in chapter 3, there has been an absence of sensory description and analysis in the social sciences. I described how Walter Ong's *The Presence of the Word* set the foundation for what has become the growing field of sensory studies. In that chapter, I described two approaches to the anthropological analysis of the sensorium: a theory-building analytical orientation to the senses and a more descriptively ethnographic representation of sensoria, which is the tack I have used in my own writing on the senses and social life. It is also the approach I've taken here on this exegesis on taste in social life.

Within the context of a multifaceted sensorial anthropology, taste is perhaps the most difficult sense to describe. In many languages there is a dearth of words that one can use to describe taste, which has both physiological and symbolic dimensions. "Recorded opinions about the sense of taste are filled with ambivalence and paradox. Some theorists consider it beneath consideration; others recommend its cultivation. Some regard taste as a mere matter of physical sensation, unworthy of extensive attention; others devote a lifetime to its exploration. Some classify taste as a lower bodily sense, along with smell and touch; others consider it as complex and informative as vision and hearing. Approaches to taste may be ascetic or sybaritic, dismissive or obsessed—and all attitudes in between."[2]

The literature on taste is therefore broad and diverse. There are many studies on the physiology of taste as well as flavoring practices in particular culinary traditions.[3] There are historical studies on the development of culinary tastes into high and low cuisines and how they create social distinction.[4] The gustatory properties of food have also been associated with religious practices. In some societies, food is linked to deities and/or saints, and is part and parcel of fasting and feasting events.[5] Perhaps the most common association of taste devolves from Immanuel Kant's *Critique of Judgment* in which the gustatory sense becomes aestheticized as it is removed from the complex and messy elements of its production. From the Kantian perspective, taste becomes a standard of refined distinction in art and in social life. Beyond Kantian dimensions of taste, writers have published studies on the cultivation of taste.[6]

Where do ethnographically contoured anthropological works fit into the broad and vast literature on taste? Very few anthropologists have considered the physiology of taste in the classic tradition of Brillat-Savarin. Fewer still have engaged in exploring the science of taste and smell or the flavoring practices of distinctive cuisines. The vast literature on the history of gustation in society has sparked some anthropological interest as in Jack Goody's sociocultural analysis of high and low cuisine, in which he charts the connection between presence of high cuisine and social hierarchy—a concrete manifestation of social inequality.

Taste has also prompted some of the more important anthropological investigations of social memory.

Perhaps the most focused anthropological takes on taste underscore how it can be extended into the realm of cultural symbolism. Several anthropologists have focused on how particular aspects of taste (strong/bitter/sweet and sour/spicy [hot and mild]). Following the careful ethnographic analysis of Mary Weismantel, we know that among Quechua-speaking people who live in Zumbahua in the Ecuadorian Andes, local terms that reference the taste sensations of strong/bitter and hot/sweet enable people "to place foods in a cultural context that shapes how people know them, creating implicit connections between sensory experience, cultural knowledge and the political and economic structures of social life."[7] Weismantel goes on to suggest that the taste sensations of sweetness and saltiness cut to the heart of gender relations in that society. Consider the specificity of taste in Weismantel's contrast of "bitter" or "strong" foods, or in Quechua, *jayaj*, to *mishqui*, which means "sweet and tasty." Strong bitter foods are eaten raw and linked to male domains outside the household, whereas sweet and tasty foods are prepared (cooked) and eaten in the house. In essence, the gustatory properties of foods are associated with gendered classifications and relate to gendered productive activities. Put another way, taste in Zumbahua is used symbolically to create and reinforce ordered cosmological categories that give shape to social practices and to social life.[8]

In the celebrated work of the late Sidney Mintz, taste becomes an active ingredient of political and economic distinction. Unlike the orientation of Bourdieu, or for that matter Kant, Mintz considers how the properties of one gustatory element—sweetness—have had an impact on social identity and changes in the perception of social class and modern consumerist individualism. As he wrote: "The first sweetened cup of hot tea to be drunk by an English worker was a significant historical event, because it prefigured the transformation of an entire society, a total remaking of its economic and social basis."[9] In his state-of-the-art paper on food, taste, and the senses, David Sutton comments on Mintz's contribution to an anthropology of taste: "Mintz develops these ideas in tracing the relationship of sugar and sweetness to moral ideas. The addictive taste of sugar made it difficult to give up, and, thus, a contentious item of anti-slavery boycott, whereas its taste once again led commentators to suggest it would lead the working classes into idleness and women into other desires and illicit pleasures."[10]

As Sutton suggests, Mintz focused on a particular flavor as a jumping-off point for understanding society and its transformations. He goes on to demonstrate how this important orientation connects with the work of C. Nadia Seremetakis and Jane Cowen, both of whom considered the impact of sweetness on Greek social life.[11] The anthropological study of taste also compels us to consider synesthesia—the dynamic blending of the senses. In chapter 3 I mentioned the work of Barbara Kirshenblatt-Gimblett, who stressed how synesthesia is central to the human experience of taste.[12]

In the end one can say that the scholars of taste do analyze the history and aestheticization of taste as well as the relation of taste (and flavor) to social identity and social change. They also consider the sensuous dynamics of taste and how they relate to phenomena like synesthesia. And yet, the scholars of taste have not fully developed their work. As Sutton concluded:

> The deployment of recent, intertwining approaches from the anthropology of the senses, phenomenology, materiality studies, and

theories of value, among others, provides exciting opportunities for rich ethnographic elaboration. And the focus on sensory aspects experienced like few other things both inside and outside of bodies (and transformed in the crossing of bodily boundaries) means that these approaches have much to gain from an engagement with food. But our theoretical progress has yet to be matched by any corpus of rich ethnographies that make the sensory aspects of food central to an understanding of lives and experiences; many of the writings on this topic remain in the form of short, suggestive articles or snippets of ethnography in larger works on other topics.[13]

Like Sutton I believe that anthropologists have just begun to sample the tastes of social worlds. To write tasteful ethnographies, anthropologists might engage in what I've been calling slow anthropology, which is, of course, increasingly difficult to practice in a fast world. The anthropology of taste fits well into the ever-expanding matrix of slowness—especially when it comes to studies of taste-in-culture.[14] As the works of Mary Weismantel, Sidney Mintz, C. Nadia Seremetakis, and David Sutton have demonstrated, it takes many years to develop the ethnographic sensitivities to understand the significant symbolic social and political dynamics of taste-in-the-world. It is through a slowly developed anthropology that one can understand how taste can bring harmony as well as disharmony to social worlds.

My slow approach to anthropology gave me the time to develop some of the sensitivities needed to understand how playing with sauces could create and undermine social harmony in Adamu Jenitongo's Tillabéri compound. On subsequent visits to Tillabéri the quality of the food did not improve. The principal compound cook, Djenaba, continued to produce mediocre food, but given the stubborn strictness of Songhay cultural protocols about family life, no one dared to take her place. During one of my visits, my mentor's older son, Moussa, ate his dinners in town and arranged for his father's sister's daughter, Ramatu, to prepare afternoon meals. He made sure that that food was shared with me and his father. For Moussa, marriage seemed like the only solution to the family's food problem. When he soon thereafter got married, his new wife, now the youngest in-law in the compound, replaced Djenaba as the family cook. Her thick savory sauces brought tasteful harmony and a long-absent sense of well-being to the Tillabéri compound.

In previous chapters I have considered how the slowly developed exploration of the senses might enhance ethnographic description, bringing to vivid life the sounds, smells, tastes, and textures of people and place. This sensuous exploration helped prepare me for my most profound ethnographic challenges in the world of Songhay sorcery: a brute introduction to the mind-bending imponderables of the bush, the wild and dangerous spaces that extend beyond the edge of Songhay villages. In the next chapter I describe incomprehensible encounters in and on the edge of the Songhay bush, a stark confrontation in a space between things. These experiences compelled me to unlearn my orientation to the world in order to better understand the relation of the village to the bush and come to grips with things, to quote Jean Rouch, "not yet known to us."[15]

Part II

EVOKING INDIGENOUS WISDOM

Today you are learning about us, but to understand
us, you'll have to grow old with us

Adamu Jenitongo

5

Peripheral Knowledge and the Imponderables of the Between

Cimi fonda: a ga cuu
Truth's path is tall (and long)

Songhay saying

During my long apprenticeship Adamu Jenitongo would often send me into the bush to look for medicinal plants. As I have mentioned in previous chapters, he lived at the edge at the village far from the center of Tillabéri. Leaving his compound of two-room rectangular mud brick houses and conical straw huts, I'd exit the village and walk into the bush.

The first time he sent me on such a mission, my teacher asked me to look for curative plants.

"How do I know where to go? How do I know what to look for?"

The old man smiled at me. "Follow the path," he said, "and you'll find your way."

I, of course, worried that I'd wander off to some godforsaken place and never be seen again.

My teacher seemed unconcerned. "Be careful in the bush," he told me. "It's a dangerous place." He chuckled. "You'll be fine."

Taking every precaution, I embarked on my first plant-seeking foray into the bush. With an empty burlap sack slung over my shoulder, I trekked east and south along laterite plains that pan-caked to distant buttes rising majestically in the Sahelian heat haze. I followed paths that cut through patches of scrub and crossed shallow wadies shaped through powerful rainy season runoff that had cut through clay and sand. In a particularly broad and deep wadi, I found plants growing in moist sandy soil—a trace of the now-distant rainy season. Having found my way, I returned with a sack full of medicinal plants.

"We'll dry these plants and use them to heal people," Adamu Jenitongo told me. "It's good you returned before darkness. The bush," he reminded me with a broad smile that converted his aged leathery face into a patchwork of wrinkles, "is dangerous."

My teacher, who died more than thirty years ago, was a *sohanci*, a healer who traced his descent patrilineally to Sonni Ali Ber, the

FIGURE 8
The Songhay bush. © Paul Stoller.

great fifteenth-century Songhay king who was renowned for his sorcerous power. Knowledge of Ali Ber's powerful practices has long been passed down to his descendants, including, of course, Adamu Jenitongo.

As a sorcerous practitioner who can heal and harm people, the sohanci is a figure who lives at the existential edge of things. He or she is the intermediary between village and bush, between the social and spirit worlds, between health and illness, and between life and death. The sohanci's familiar is the vulture (*zeyban*), a creature that partakes of the dead to live in the present. The vulture represents substantial power and mystery; it flies high and travels great distances. To emulate their familiar, sohanci, who have been known to fly great distances in the dark of night, usually wear black. Like the vulture, they present themselves as mysterious beings who are feared and respected.[1]

Like his father and his father's father, Adamu Jenitongo always lived far from the center of the village. In the Songhay world no one wants to live close to a sohanci for fear of her or his overabundance of power, a force that can burn those who get too close. And so, the sohanci is a peripheral figure par excellence. He or she lives a life filled with what John Keats long ago called "negative capability," the capacity to live with incompleteness and contradiction.[2] In the arena of negative capability, one is compelled to pay attention and accept the experiential state of "not knowing your frontside," to quote a Songhay incantation, "from your backside." In such a place one brutally confronts the limits of comprehension.

Consider a "not-knowing-your-frontside-from-your-backside" event that I experienced at the edge of the village. I had been living in my teacher's dune-top compound for almost two months. My mentor had been teaching me about the curative properties of plants, knowledge he would only convey to me in *cino bi*, "the black of night," which meant that I often felt sleep-deprived. One night after a black-of-night session, braying donkeys and howling dogs woke me from a fitful sleep. As I got up from my bed, the brays and howls grew louder, heading in my direction. As I approached the closed door, I heard footsteps and high-pitched vocalizations—a kind of strange gibberish. Then came the screechy scrapes of fingernails on corrugated tin—my door. Frozen in place, I wanted to open the door but lacked the courage to do so. The screechy scrapes continued, followed by a high-pitched whine that sounded like a child's voice. Slowly the sounds moved away, as did the donkey brays and dog howls. Stealing all the courage I could muster, I opened the door. A ribbon of dawn orange stretched across the eastern horizon. At the edge of the bush, I saw dogs leaping the in air.

Moments later I woke my teacher's son and asked him if he had heard anything.

"No, I didn't hear anything," he said.

Needing verification, I approached Adamu Jenitongo and told him what I had experienced.

"You heard it, too?"

"Yes, Baba, what was it?"

"The *Atakurma* came to visit."

"The little people—guardians of the bush?" I asked.

"You heard their squeaky little voices, and the dogs and donkeys?" He paused. "The dogs and donkeys get excited when they come."

My teacher explained that on Sundays, a day of the spirits, he would usually take a bowl of honey or milk into the bush and leave it for the Atakurma. "It's been some time since I last brought them an offering. They came for honey or milk." He shook his head. "You heard that?"

What I heard brought me to the edge of comprehension.

Had my senses betrayed me? Had I been dreaming?

Could the Atakurma be more than a sleep-deprived hallucination?

In the immediate aftermath of that turbulent situation, I remembered that Adamu Jenitongo had once told me that human beings, who live in the village, cannot control the wild forces of the bush. To understand the bush, he counseled, you must surrender to it and let it penetrate your being—a transformative process fraught with personal risk and existential vulnerability. Faced with a similar kind of philosophical incomprehension, as I suggested in the introduction, the great nineteenth-century philosopher Friedrich Nietzsche offered some advice about how to absorb the disturbing particularities of not-knowing—the remedy of art.

Consider the existential dilemmas evoked in a Sufi story about an old man who is called to visit his ailing friend who lives in a different village. To get there the old man must cross a rickety footbridge that spans a deep gorge through which a raging river kicks up a menacing display of white water. The old man, who has long harbored a fear of heights, approached the footbridge with no small amount of trepidation. The wind kicked up, rocking the footbridge from side to side, which increased exponentially the old man's fear of heights and the threat of a lethal fall into the gorge.

Would they ever find his mangled body downriver?

And yet, he knew that his friend had been stricken with a potentially fatal illness, which meant that he had to see him. That resolve pushed him onto the bridge. His weight made the footbridge creak and sway. Once he was on the footbridge the wind whipped him from side to side. Fearful, he held on and looked down—into the void. His head spun. Behind him was his past, a known space from where he came. Before him was his future, an unknown place to where he was going. In this unsettled state, his mind suddenly cleared. Sparked with an unanticipated jolt of energy and creativity, he crossed to the other side and envisioned a fresh world filled with new possibilities.

For Sufi masters like Ibn al-Arabi, the twelfth-century Andalusian mystic, the old man on the wind-whipped footbridge had experienced *barzakh*, that which connects two things that had been separate—health and illness, life and death, the social and spirit world. For Ibn al-Arabi, crossing a footbridge that connects two worlds positioned the old man in *the between*, a place of existential risk that also inspires creativity and renewal, a space that ultimately provokes fundamental change.

When you do anthropology, you are sometimes compelled to stretch your imagination to the limits of comprehension—and beyond. If you allow the imagination to stretch with experience, especially when confronted with the ineffability of something like a frightening walk on a rickety footbridge, a sudden confrontation with death, or an early morning encounter with the Atakurma, you can find yourself in the between. The philosopher N. J. T. Thomas suggested that "the principal reason that the imagination is thought to be particularly relevant to the arts arises from the ability of artists to see and to induce the rest of us to see aspects of reality differently or more fully than is ordinary—to see things—as we otherwise might not."[3]

Such an orientation to the imagination is often linked to religious beliefs and to what William James called "radical empiricism"—the sensing of the unseen. The great scholar of Sufism, William Chittick, following the insights of William James, among others, wrote about the importance of the imagination in Islamic belief and practice. "In putting complete faith in reason," he suggested, "the West forgot that imagination opens the soul to certain possibilities of perceiving and understanding not available to the rational mind. . . . By granting an independent ontological status to imagination and seeing the visionary realm as the self-revelation of God, Islamic philosophy has gone against the mainstream of Western thought."[4] The impulse of the imagination enables you to follow a path leading toward a truth of being, a space between things.

In Sufi thought the barzakh, the space between things, figures prominently in the works of Ibn al-Arabi, who wrote that the between is

> something that separates . . . two other things, while never going to one side . . . as for example, the line that separates shadow from sun light. God says, "he let forth the two seas that meet together, between them a barzakh they do not overpass (Koran 55:19); in other words one sea does not mix with the other. . . . Any two adjacent things are in need of barzakh, which is neither one or the other but which possesses the power . . . of both. The barzakh is something that separates a known from an unknown, an existent from a non-existent, a negated from an affirmed, and intelligible from a non-intelligible.[5]

Vincent Crapanzano wrote evocatively about the cultural and philosophical significance of the between.

> If we take the imagination, as Sartre and in his own way Ibn al-'Arabi do, as presenting that which is absent or nonexistent, we have to conclude that it is through an activity, which rests on the nonbeing of its object—the image—that we uncover those gaps, those disjunctive moments of nonbeing, that punctuate our social and cultural life. The imagination also provides us with the glosses, the rhetorical devices, the narrative maneuvers, and the ritual strategies to conceal those gaps. We uncover, as it were, nonbeing

through an act that postulates nonbeing, as we conceal that nonbeing through a nonbeing we declare, in ritual at least, to have full being—plenitude. What is more "real" than objects of ritual? . . . Is it this paradox that leads to the continual (if repetitive) elaborations in ritual and drama, in literature and art, especially and most purely in music, of the asymptotic moment of crossing, that renders imaginative frontiers so menacing as they fascinate and enchant us? Such subterfuge, if one may call it so, is a source of unending social and cultural creativity—or its cessation—through repetition and the declaration of that repetition as ultimate truth.[6]

Following this line of thought, the imagination's artistic exuberance compels us, like the old man on the rickety footbridge, to wake up and see the world from fresh perspectives. This notion follows the sage advice of Jean Rouch, who liked to say that the imagination compels us to tell stories, which give birth to other stories. As I once suggested, "the imagination always brings us back to the story."[7] These are often tales about events that "at least for the moment cannot be explained and can barely be described."[8]

Songhay elders like to say: if your path is good, it will be a long and tall one that takes many years to navigate. That path continuously leads you to crossroads that separate one world from another. Adamu Jenitongo spent much of his life wandering the spaces that stretch out between things. He was born in Jesse, a town famous for its magical lake, its sorcery, and its witchcraft. His father, Jenitongo Seyni, was a red sohanci, a direct descendant of Sonni Ali Ber through both his father and mother. Sonni Ali Ber was the Songhay sorcerer king who ruled over the Songhay empire from 1464 to 1491. People thought that Adamu Jenitongo's mother was a witch (*cerkaw*), which meant that my teacher would be considered a white sohanci—only one parent linked directly to the Songhay emperor. If a sohanci is partially a witch, he can become a *guunu*, one of a select group of practitioners who perform circumcisions. In West Africa, circumcisions are events laced with existential implication. As a result, they require a specialist of broad and deep personal power.

By the time he was in his late teens Adamu Jenitongo began to perform circumcisions. At first, he performed them relatively close to home, but soon news of his skill spread far and wide. Because the power and reputation of the sohanci was well known in West Africa, it was not surprising that the demands for my mentor's services came from Burkina Faso, Benin, Togo, and Côte d'Ivoire—well beyond the lands of the Songhay.

Here's how it worked. Young Adamu would leave his home in Jesse and ride his horse to the west. Dressed in sohanci black (drawstring trousers, tunic, boubou, and turban), he'd ride for many kilometers across vast tawny plains of scrub bush, black rocks, and thorn trees that extended to sandstone buttes, that in turn, gave way to more scrub bush and rocky plains. The monotony of this desiccated landscape would be broken by clusters of green that marked a pond, where he'd come upon a village—a swirl of conical mud brick huts with thatch roofs. There Songhay villagers would celebrate the arrival of the black-clad visitor on a black stallion—the sohanci guunu had arrived. The village boys would immediately water and feed his horse. Village elders would welcome him with deep respect—for his power and his skill—and show him to the place, usually a small mud brick hut with a thatch roof, where he'd perform his operation. The young boys would present themselves, one by one. My teacher would speak to them softly to calm their nerves, recite an incantation that brought harmony to the world, and quickly remove the boy's foreskin. He then would apply two herbal salves—one that disinfected the wound and one that dulled the pain. He'd then tell the young man to retire to his house, eat well, and rest for three days. After he had circumcised all the eligible boys, the elders would kill and roast a sheep or a goat. In the evening they would feast. After sleeping in that village, he'd collect a modest fee the next morning and be on his way, always to the west, where he'd find the next village in need of his skills.

When Adamu Jenitongo journeyed south and west, he eventually left the laterite steppes of his native Sahel, descended a steep escarpment, and ventured into the savannah. There he followed dirt paths lined with tall elephant grass and cottonwood trees. In his youth this grassland was lion country, and the people who lived there, mostly Mossi, Gurma, Bobo, and Bwa, spoke languages that my mentor did not understand. Even so, these people recognized the powerful reputation of the Songhay sohanci. Despite his relative youth, they treated the young visitor with no small degree of reverence.

These groups tended to live in elaborately constructed mud brick villages the dwellings of which featured ornate geometric designs. In these villages the moment of circumcision required much preparation and ceremony. The elders of these villages would gather in a central location massing hundreds of candidates, some as young as five, some as old as fifteen. Armed with his scalpel and his herbal salves, Adamu Jenitongo would circumcise a hundred or more boys in one day. At sunset, the elders would butcher a cow and, in honor of my teacher's presence, would stage a feast during which the villagers ate beef and drank millet beer (*chapalo*) into the wee hours. After a night of rest, the young sohanci would mount his black stallion and make his way to the next village.

In time, the traveling circumciser returned home to Jesse, where, in the campfire's flickering light, he'd recount the tale of his journey to the strange lands to the south and west where people ate bushmeat and drank millet beer. When his relatives criticized such behavior, my teacher, wise beyond his years, reminded them that just like the Songhay, these people were all *Adam'izo*—the offspring of Adam. From an early age, then, my teacher experienced barzakh, the curious space between language, culture, ecology, and cultural practice—an existential experience from which he extracted a degree of wisdom.

His father, Jenitongo Seyni, sent him on these trips so that his son and successor might understand the power of the between. Following the millet harvest Adamu Jenitongo continued his circumcision treks to the south and west. He did so without complaint or complication. His father had long known that his son possessed the even disposition necessary to bear the burdens of possessing the power to maim, sicken, or kill. When Jenitongo Seyni neared death, he summoned his son to his bedside. With his last breath, the old sohanci revealed to his son the *gindize gina*, the magic word imbued with the great power of his sorcerer ancestors. It is a word that is only revealed at the moment of death. Just then, Jenitongo Seyni vomited three small chains (*sisiri*) onto his chest. With that last act, the esteemed sorcerer died. With great difficulty Adamu Jenitongo gathered the chains into his hands and swallowed them. In so doing, he became his father's successor, which meant that people in the region feared and revered him. His new status also meant that rivals would test the limits of his power.

Soon after becoming his father's successor, my mentor married. In short order he fathered a son and daughter, both of whom died shortly after their births. Meanwhile, a man in Jesse had a not-so-secret affair with the new sohanci's wife. When villagers found the decapitated body of the man in his millet field, the man's family accused Adamu Jenitongo of the murderous crime. In 1937 the colonial police came to Jesse, arrested Adamu Jenitongo, and took him west to a military prison in Tillabéri, where he waited three years for his trial to convene in colonial court. During that time the prisoners worked in rice fields and built roads. From time to time the authorities let Adamu Jenitongo's family visit him. They brought him his favorite meals, which bolstered his spirits.

At the trial my teacher professed his innocence, but the prosecutor described him as a murderous sorcerer who should be banished from Niger. Convinced by this prosecutorial case, the French judge found him guilty. In 1940 he condemned the alleged murderer to a military prisoner camp in Chidal, a desolate place deep in the Sahara. There my teacher worked as a roadbuilding laborer. But Adamu Jenitongo used his sohanci skills to survive. After two years of hard labor, the commander of the prison made him a cook in the officer's mess.

During that time, he learned French and began to understand the machinations of a French military outpost-prison. The French military eventually transferred him to Post Maurice Cortier, also known as Bidon 5, an infamous military prison camp in a particularly desolate part of the Sahara. The heat, wind, and lack of adequate water and food made a prison tenure at Bidon 5 a likely death sentence. But my teacher, who continued to cook for the officers, survived that ordeal. He remained at Bidon 5 for one year, after which the commandant transferred him to Tessalit, another French military prison in Mali, where he also cooked for the officers.

By the end of the war Commandant Villey made him the head cook of the officer's mess. Never in his life had he seen so much food—cabbage, onions, and more meat than he could imagine. In the postwar years he continued to cook for the Tessalit officers. Because they liked him, the officers quietly encouraged him to save food for himself and his fellow cooks. They also gave Adamu Jenitongo his own house.

As the years rolled by the relatively rich diet of the officer's mess produced physical changes. The sohanci, who had always been short and slight, took on a more rotund shape. The French officers eventually asked my teacher, now seen as a rotund, kindhearted elder, to be the caretaker of their children. During the last years of his confinement, he spent most of his time in the officers' living quarters. He drank their water, had access to their medicines, and ate what they ate, which meant lots of meat.

In 1960 Mali and Niger became independent nations. In response France released the Malian and Nigerien prisoners who had been condemned to French military camps. Commandant Villey gave his head cook release papers to present to local authorities on his arrival in Niger. He also gave him 5,000 francs for spending money and a bus ticket for his return home. Before Adamu Jenitongo's departure Commandant Villey gifted him a bolt of beautiful blue damask cloth and told his head cook to go to a local tailor who could produce for him an elegant grand boubou—an embroidered flowing robe, with matching shirt and trousers.

After roughly twenty years in French military camps, Adamu Jenitongo, whose age now made him a Songhay elder, began his trek back to his former life. Commandant Villey sent word of my teacher's imminent return to family members in Tillabéri, who had long thought their kinsman had died during confinement. The homecoming bus made its way slowly along the rutted roads south of Gao. Acacia thorns had several times punctured the bus tires.

The repairs added many hours to the slow but momentous journey home. At least the driver had made sure to fill up several jerricans with petrol, which meant they avoided the troublesome burden of a *panne d'essence*. When they finally crossed the border into the new Republic of Niger, Adamu Jenitongo and the other passengers got off the bus. The former prisoner and cook took a handful of Nigerien soil and recited the *genji how*, the sohanci incantation that harmonizes the forces of the bush. Once across the border, the bus continued its southward journey along the eastern bank of the Niger River. From the road Adamu Jenitongo knowingly observed how the dull brown of the Sahelian steppe gradually flowed into rice paddy green. Beyond a cluster of small islands, home to Niger River fishermen (*sorkowa*), the western bank's ribbon of green gradually gave way to dots of scrub bush that swept up toward the summit of towering dunes.

Eventually, they arrived in Tillabéri. Dressed in his splendid blue damask boubou, Adamu Jenitongo got off the bus, but he recognized no one at the depot. He did notice a short, slight woman wandering among the welcoming crowd. Her crinkled forehead signaled concern.

"Adamu Jenitongo, where are you?" she asked loudly. "Did you miss the bus?"

Adamu Jenitongo approached his sister. "Kedibo, I am here."

"It can't be. You don't look like Adamu. You're so fat. And look at those expensive clothes." Tears streamed down her face. "We are so happy that you're alive."

"Sister, I have lived with the white man for twenty years. I cooked his food. I took care of his children. I ate his food which is why I am fat."

"You are home now," she told him. She waved to a man in the crowd. "Over here, Moussa."

A tall thin man dressed in white tunic and black trousers fashioned from thin cotton approached.

Kedibo pointed to him. "That's my husband," she said to Adamu Jenitongo.

Strangers came up to Adamu Jenitongo to introduce themselves. They had heard that a powerful sohanci who had survived twenty years in French military prisons had returned to Niger.

"We welcome you, sohanci."

"Help us make our way."

"We want you to settle here in Tillabéri."

Moussa greeted his brother-in-law. "Sohanci, we want you to stay in Tillabéri. We need you here. We have arranged a place for you to stay. It's close to the bush on top of a dune that overlooks the river."

Moussa gestured for some boys to come and gather Adamu Jenitongo's things. So began the trek to his new life as the spiritual guardian of Tillabéri. This previously exiled Songhay healer who had long journeyed on the path that wound its way between things moved into a compound at the edge of town—on the periphery of village and bush. The compound consisted of one small two-room mud brick house with a thatch roof. Next to the mud brick house stood a conical straw hut, which became the spirit house where Adamu Jenitongo placed the ritual objects that his sister had kept in her house—iron staffs, miniature sandals (for the Atakurma), large clay pots to mix potions, and an assortment of cloth bags that held medicinal herbs as well as substances used in sorcery rites. Adamu Jenitongo also put in the spirit hut an array of other ritual items—lances, hatchets, and costumes—that could be used during spirit possession ceremonies.

On learning that Adamu Jenitongo now lived in Tillabéri, people streamed to his compound for treatment. When a client

FIGURE 9
Adamu Jenitongo's spirit hut. © Paul Stoller.

presented himself or herself, he threw cowrie shells or did sand tracings (geomancy) to diagnose the source of the person's problem. Then he would mix potions, apply salves, suggest a sacrifice, or recommend that the client sponsor a ceremony to seek the aid of one of 150 Songhay spirits.

Given his reputation, people in Tillabéri encouraged him to be their *zima*, or priest of the local possession troupe. The zima's job is to organize spirit possession activities—to safeguard the health and well-being of the community. Pleased with the respect that Tillabéri people had bestowed on him, he agreed to complement his obligations as a healer with those of a spirit possession priest. In this way, the sohanci's compound at the edge of the village became the site of spirit possession ceremonies in Tillabéri.

It was evident that Adamu Jenitongo would remain in Tillabéri. Given this turn of events, the sohanci's sister, Kedibo, arranged his first marriage to Hadjo, a mild-mannered Tillabéri woman who was her husband's sister. Within a year, Hadjo gave birth to Moussa. Because all of Adamu Jenitongo's previous children had died as toddlers, he worried about his new son, but Moussa grew into a healthy child. Moussa's vitality compelled Kedibo, a very persuasive woman, to talk to her brother about marrying a woman from their hometown, Jesse. After the harvest her brother welcomed the hot-tempered Jemma into his compound. Within a year, Jemma gave birth to another son, Moru, who, like his brother Moussa, grew into an energetic young boy.

By the time he had established himself in Tillabéri, Adamu Jenitongo had traveled to the edges of his physical and emotional worlds. As a young man, he learned a great deal from other West African groups whose social and cultural practices differed from those of the Songhay. On his death, Jenitongo Seyni, his father, initiated him as a sohanci, a master practitioner who knew how to harm as well as heal. He married and sired several children, all of whom died. His enemies accused him of murdering his wife's lover, and after three years of hard labor in a Tillabéri prison, a judge condemned him to French military prisons in the Sahara. After laboring for two years, he became a cook, and eventually the head cook for the officer's mess in Chidal, Bidon 5, and Tessalit. Experience on the periphery ripened Adamu Jenitongo's mind, enabling him to negotiate the turbulent spaces that separate two worlds. This set of experiences sharpened the scope of his sorcerous power, increased his capacity to adapt to changing circumstances, and enhanced his creativity, all of which made him a formidable healer, a true spiritual guardian of his community.

More than ten years after he settled in Tillabéri, Adamu Jenitongo staged a spirit possession ceremony on his dune-top compound. The cries of the one-string violin and the clack-roll-clack of the gourd drum echoed in the dry dusty air. These seductive sounds compelled a young American who taught at the nearby secondary school to trudge up a steep dune to witness a spirit possession ceremony. My entrance into Adamu Jenitongo's compound marked the beginning of a seventeen-year journey on a peripheral path that would challenge my sensibilities, bring into relief my limitations, and shift my personal and professional priorities.

During those seventeen years Adamu Jenitongo guided me to the portal of an incompressible world, the experience of which often challenged my sense of reality.

Is it possible for spirits to take the bodies of human beings?

Can a person like Adamu Jenitongo have nocturnal conversations with his ancestors?

Can a Songhay diviner hear the voice of the Nya Beri, a spirit sound that uncovers the past, peers deeply into the present, and discovers the future?

Can Dongo, the mercurial thunder god, kill people who knowingly or unknowingly violate the sacredness of his land?

Can a practitioner's magical incantations and ritual offerings sicken or kill a person?

Can witches steal a person's soul, condemning them to chronic illness and/or death?

Can a person have a conversation with the Atakurma, the little people of the Songhay bush?

During that long journey I continuously confronted these existential questions. At first, they tormented me, forcing me to wonder about the state of my sanity. In time, I learned to open myself to Adamu Jenitongo's world in which impossibilities become possibilities, in which reason is not necessarily applicable, in which, to return once again to Nietzsche, "logic bites its own tail." Such existential wandering made me vulnerable—to the wrath of the spirits, to sorcerous attack, and to professional scorn. In truth, opening my being to the Songhay world situated me, like the old man on the wind-whipped footbridge, as a person temporarily caught between the comforts of his past, the turbulence of his present, and the uncertainty of his future.

Of course, most anthropologists have shared many of these existential dilemmas. Like Adamu Jenitongo, anthropologists have long wandered in the spaces between things. Anthropologists continuously live in social worlds of diverse language and culture. As scholars who engage in long periods of fieldwork, anthropologists become proponents of *being there*. Then they return home to a state of *being here*.[9] Indeed, some anthropologists find themselves in the nether state, following Merleau-Ponty, of being everywhere and nowhere, which powerfully defines the imponderable qualities of barzakh—being between two separate entities.[10]

Being between things shapes anthropological practice-in-the-world. Given its centrality, it is perhaps important to refine our thinking about what it means to be between things. Clearly, there is a long disciplinary history of writing about the between, especially from the analytical perspective of Victor and Edith Turner and their notions of liminality and communitas. "Liminal entities," Victor Turner wrote in his classic work, *The Ritual Process*, "are neither here nor there; they are betwixt and between the positions assigned and arrayed custom, convention, and ceremonial."[11] In that same essay Turner described the traits of people who find themselves in liminal states. He suggested people finding themselves in liminal states might be humble and willing to uncomplainingly submit to orders. Sometimes, they might submit to painful processes—ritual scarification, tests of endurance, or in the case of a cancer patient who is between health and illness, chemotherapy and/or radiation treatments. The Turner model of liminality showcased how processes of transformation propel the passage from one status to another—from child to adult, from single to married, from novice to master.

For Songhay sorcerers, liminality is usually a state without resolution. In continuous liminality, which is the lived reality of the Songhay sorcerer as well as the anthropologist, you are always in the between and can never return to your previous status. Being continuously liminal means that people may well simplistically essentialize you as an apprentice sorcerer or an anthropologist. It is also a state that often gives rise to a sense of social connection so powerful that it can undermine previously noticed differences in age, gender, social class, and ethnicity. Victor and Edith Turner referred to this state as communitas. In 2012 Edith Turner wrote that communitas "occurs through the readiness of people—perhaps from necessity—to rid themselves of their concern for status and dependence of structures and see their fellows as they are."[12] She goes on to critique an anthropology that diminishes the importance of communitas in human experience:

Anthropology has given the world a great store of scientific understanding of society, its bones and muscles, its illnesses, but it has not allowed itself to get mixed up in such matters as person-to-person feeling unless they are analyzable and unless the analysis shows some kind of objectivity about human identity and consciousness. [Turner's] book, however, tackles communitas, togetherness itself, taking the reader to the edge of the precipice of knowledge—and beyond, over the barrier of the scientists' analysis and into experience itself. Light draws on what the real thing is, and we feel lucky it exists. Then we can make discoveries.[13]

In communitas, which often results from being in a position of liminality, you step out onto the wind-whipped footbridge and experience the trials, tribulations, and revelations of barzakh—of being always already between things.

People who practice anthropology live in the between. Such an unstable vantage might at first glance seem disadvantageous or troublesome. But closer inspection of these existential dynamics pushes us inexorably toward the margin of things, a place of enormous creative potential. Bruce Kapferer has termed this turbulent positionality "Guerrilla Anthropology." In an interview in the *University of Bergen Magazine* Kapferer said:

To me, in a sense, guerrilla anthropology is anthropology. Anthropology stands outside all of disciplines. To put it crudely, most of the disciplines practiced at universities have been born in the Nineteenth Century and in the history of nationalism, which began the modern state. . . . Many unexamined assumptions regarding the nature and possibility of human beings were present that required challenge. Western philosophy offered a radical critique but it, nonetheless, could not escape the limitation of many assumptions that were culturally and historically embedded in it. . . . But anthropology also took seriously other systems. These other systems were not necessarily bound by the same principles or frameworks of understanding that our own worlds were. Anthropology is a guerrilla discipline in the sense that it comes from outside a largely Western comprehension of things and challenges ruling assumptions. . . . The critical guerrilla anthropological perspective will lead to important reassessments of conceptual and theoretical perspectives that are still dominating discussions on problems associated with inequality.[14]

Most of the guerrilla anthropologists I've met understand that the old colonialist ways of solving social problems or understanding the world don't work anymore. Our various systems of politics, economics, and scholarship have become ineffectual and counterproductive. In this context, the guerrilla approach to anthropology, which emerges from long-standing experience in the between, is perfectly suited to living in, understanding, and coping with the crises that shape contemporary social worlds.

Kapferer's approach, which is the orientation I embrace in this book, takes us to the periphery of things—to the edge of consciousness. It challenges us to invent new forms to consider social worlds from perspectives freed from what Clifford Geertz long ago called the "dead hand of competence."[15] Indeed, a new generation of anthropologists have concluded that past methods are out of sync with a world tuned to a new set of frequencies. Confronted with contemporary social complexities, the new generation embraces them rather than attempting to reduce complexity to a logically coherent set of formulae. Consider the group of emerging scholars who contributed to the previously mentioned 2021 anthology *Peripheral Methodologies: Unlearning, Not-knowing, and Ethnographic Limits*. It is a collection of stunningly creative and thoughtful essays, all of which evoke the remedy of art to probe the indeterminate gray light that illuminates the spaces between things. These anthropologists suggest the remedy of art to highlight the process of unlearning on the path to artisanal mastery. They suggest the remedy of art to confront ethnographic reality in the absence of knowledge.[16]

Between the lines of these elegant essays, the contributors realize what it takes to understand the power of the bush, to comprehend artisanal skill, and to describe an ethnographic event or film an ethnographic scene. They demonstrate that deep listening and deep comprehension come not from disembodied theorization but from opening their bodies to the world in much the way that a painter, returning once again to Merleau-Ponty's *Eye and Mind*, uses body and being to create a tableau.

In the conclusion to their edited collection, Martínez, Di Puppo, and Frederiksen think about how peripheral methodologies carry us toward spaces of peripheral knowledge. Here's what they say about the notion of peripheral knowledge.

> Rather than leading to a sharpness of vision, the peripheral methodologies we discover in our field experiences can be thought of as leading to a sharpness of attention. The Greek mētis that appears in Klekot's text on pottery is knowledge in movement, a knowledge that espouses the shifting quality of a moving world, but it is also full alertness, the capacity to be fully aware of the present moment. As much as Varvantakis drifts away in dreamy abandonment when savouring a dish during his fieldwork (one that unexpectedly brings him back to his grandmother's kitchen), the details that the dish brings to mind are potent in their liveliness. While peripheral wisdom is about engaging with indistinctiveness and discontinuity—the inherent vagueness of phenomena and field experiences, which seem to hang between the known and the unknown—it also brings about vividness and sharpness in the mode of attention that results from it. It is akin to seeing things anew, in a perpetual discovery of the world. When engaging with

associations and constellations that appear incoherent, out of place, or with subtle moments and experiences that may appear to lack "relevance," we become fully engaged in our field, fully alert to the way things present themselves to us. This state of alertness is also humility in the presence of the unknown and of the enduring mystery of the world we encounter.[17]

During fieldwork in Tillabéri, Niger, I witnessed scores of spirit possession ceremonies. At the time, I did not know how my witnessing would affect my personal and professional life. But the music, the old words of spirit praise songs, and the image of old women, spirit mediums all, moving to the sacred sound focused my gaze on their faces—especially their eyes, which seemed to burn with passion for the music, for the dance, and for the spirits.

At one ceremony, however, the spirits chose not to possess their mediums. As the sun gradually dipped toward the western horizon producing swirls of pink and rose-colored clouds, a spirit from the east, a female Doguwa, came into the body of a powerfully built male medium, who stripped off his shirt and tied a strip of Dutch wax cloth—red and black blocks of color offset by images of blooming yellow flowers—around his head.

"I am a woman," the spirit in the body of medium bellowed as she/he strutted about the dance grounds. "I am a woman."

Violent Hauka spirits took the bodies of two other mediums. They foamed at the mouth. They pounded their chests, grunted, and groaned.

I had seated myself next to the spirit possession drummers under the ceremonial canopy. This vantage gave me a very good look at the physical transformations that occur when spirits colonize a medium's body. Suddenly the Doguwa spirit strutted over toward me. Smoke rose from the contents of a gourd he was holding.

"I have hot ash for the *anasaara* [white man]."

I froze.

"Stand up and accept your gift."

I stood up and the Doguwa spirit dumped the hot ash on my head. Everyone cheered.

"You have been blessed," a man said to me. "That spirit will look out for you."

I didn't feel blessed. My scalp throbbed. I abandoned my hot, sweaty spot under the ceremonial hangar and made my way to the dance grounds. As soon as I did, one of the Hauka, in the body of another powerfully built male medium, grabbed my arm and stared at me with blazing eyes. He looked into my eyes and sprayed me with saliva. Holding on to my arm, he spoke to me in a mixture of pidgin French and Songhay.

"We are the same," he said. "Both European." Saliva frothed from his mouth and caked on his chin. "You need to do something before you leave Niger."

Not knowing what to say or do, I asked: "What do I need to do?"

"You need to buy a box of sugar cubes and give them to the children in this part of town. Save three cubes for yourself."

"Why do that?" I asked the Hauka.

Between guttural grunts and boisterous bellows, he said: "In the name of Bonji [God], take those cubes and keep them until you get on the airplane [*bene hi* or canoe of the sky] that will take you home. When you leave the ground, take those sugar cubes, and throw them over your left shoulder. Do that and your work, like the bene hi, will rise to the heavens."

When the sun set the spirits slipped out of the bodies of their exhausted mediums and I told Adamu Jenitongo what had transpired between me and the Hauka spirit.

"When a spirit tells you to do something," he said, "don't think about it. Just do it."

"But how can I throw three sugar cubes over my left shoulder in the crowded cabin of an airborne plane?"

"You'll find a way," my mentor said. "You'll be fine."

My teacher's words reminded me of his advice on finding medicinal plants in the dangerous bush. You'll find a way, he had told me.

Here was yet another moment of being between things. Should I react to the experience as a trained anthropologist seeking to discover the truth of spirit possession, which, following the rules of logic, cannot exist, or should I slip into the consciousness of the Songhay world and do what the Hauka spirit told me to do? That evening I went to a neighborhood dry goods shop and bought a box of sugar. The next day I wandered about the *quartier* to distribute sugar cubes.

"Sukar ne ha," I chanted. Children came running, their hands outstretched. In short order, I had given away 247 cubes to some very happy kids. As instructed, I retained three cubes for myself—all to throw over my left shoulder after takeoff. Why should I, a young scholar, perform such a patently ridiculous act? Besides, could such a ritual act really have a direct impact on my professional life?

To return home, I first had to take a Niamey-to-Paris flight that departed at midnight. With three sugar cubes secured in a baggy that I strategically placed in the left front pocket of my trousers, I checked my bags, paid the ticket agent a small bribe for a better seat, got my ticket, cleared customs and passport control, and walked out onto the tarmac. I settled into an aisle seat in the rear cabin of the DC-10. Soon thereafter, we took off. When the captain turned off the seat belt sign, I stood up and walked to the back of the plane and entered one of two lavatories. Securing the door, I positioned my back in front of the toilet, took out the three cubes of sugar, placed them in my left hand, and recited a *genji how* to harmonize the forces of the bush. I then threw the cubes over my left shoulder. They landed in the toilet where they quickly dissolved. I returned to my seat feeling a bit foolish but also triumphant. From that moment to the present, I feel that the Hauka spirits have my back.

In the background of my consciousness, thoughts of my anthropological training tempted me to step back from that experiential periphery so I might dispassionately analyze its elements, its systemicity, and its cohesiveness. For me, the impact of that moment of unlearning and not-knowing unveiled the limits of ethnography. For me, the surreal texture of my Hauka experience required the remedy of art. As the old man in the Sufi parable came to understand, the existential turbulence of the footbridge sharpens our comprehension of the past and enables us to move toward the future with confident determination. In the between we find at the edge of the village we are better able to find the story.

And if we find the story, we also find ourselves.

Stories, of course, can take on many forms. Some are straightforward. Others are sinewy and convoluted. Many stories are laced with serious reflection; other stories are filled with humor. There are tales that convey a heavy pathos and others that are creatively lighthearted. The substance of a tale compels the storyteller to structure her or his narrative in a certain fashion. There is no formula for crafting a story, but most of the stories that provoke us to listen, read, or watch, as I articulated in the introduction, feature the evocation of space/place, the presence of energetic dialogue, and the formulation of nuanced portraits of character. In the next chapter, I describe the essential elements in Jean Rouch's rules of storytelling. Rouch used the remedy of art to confront and respond to the social and cultural disruptions of colonialism and racism in the mid-twentieth century.

6

The World According to Rouch

Kumba hinka ga charotarey numey
"It takes two hands to nourish a friendship."

Songhay proverb

It was 8:30 a.m. and I sat at a table in the Bal Bullier, a historic café on the Boulevard Montparnasse in Paris's fourteenth arrondissement. I had made an appointment with Jean Rouch to interview him about his early research and filmmaking in the Republic of Niger. When I arrived, Rouch, of course, was not there. He was always late. He liked to say to people, "Je suis ponctuellement en retard," which translates roughly to "I am punctually late," a curious and ironic statement. Knowing that Rouch was "punctually late," I brought reading material, an ethnography and a mystery novel, to pass the time until his arrival. To my great surprise Jean Rouch showed up at 8:45.

"Jean," I said. "You're so early!"

"I wanted to get a good start on your topic, Paul. I like talking about my time among the sorcerers of Wanzerbe."

Rouch insisted on ordering two large bowls of café au lait and a basket of croissants, which he insisted were the best in Paris. "If we are to talk about serious matters, like filming Songhay sorcerers in Wanzerbe, Niger, in 1947, we must have good coffee and good croissants."

As we began to eat, I noticed a woman walking toward our table. She carried what looked like a bound manuscript.

"Monsieur Rouch?" she asked.

"Oui?"

"We have an appointment for 8:30. I've come all the way from Martinique to see you about my manuscript."

Rouch slapped his forehead, looked at me, and shrugged his shoulders. "I forgot, Paul. She's come all way form Martinique. I have to go, but I'll be back. Order more coffee and croissants."

I sipped a fresh bowl of café au lait, continued to eat the buttery croissants, and dove into my mystery novel. One hour later, Rouch returned to the table. He ordered more coffee and croissants. As we prepared to talk about his early films in Niger, a tall gentleman approached. He too carried a bound manuscript.

"Monsieur Rouch?"

"Oui?"

"We have an appointment for 10:00 a.m. I've come from Germany for my thesis defense. You are on my jury." He paused. "The defense is Friday."

Jean Rouch slapped his forehead again. "Bon Dieu! Paul," he said as he smiled at me. "I forgot. His defense is in two days. I have to meet with him. I'll be back."

Rouch returned at lunchtime and sat down.

"Lunch?" he asked. "Let's get some white wine spritzers, and the veal here is excellent."

At lunch we sipped, ate, and bantered about the Songhay people, our mutual friends in Niger, and the state of French anthropology.

"It's time to talk," he said. "Take out your tape recorder."

It was the beginning of a fabulous conversation about Wanzerbe, the fabled village of Songhay sorcerers, the film *Les magiciens de Wanzerbe* (1947), the great sorcerer Mossi Bana, and four legendary filmmakers: Jean Cocteau, Jean Renoir, Jean-Luc Godard, and François Truffaut. Time slipped away. When I glanced outside, it was beginning to get dark.

"Dinner?"

"This has been terrific, Jean, but I can't."

"Neither can I. I've already missed many appointments. But today was a good day, was it not?"

It had been a memorable day. I recorded material that would eventually appear in *The Cinematic Griot*, my book on the ethnography of Jean Rouch. But I also learned something important about Jean Rouch's approach to the world. For Rouch, anthropologists and filmmakers need to be fully engaged in the moment. The rationale of such full engagement, as I later learned, comes from the Songhay notion about patience. If you are fully engaged and patient, the Songhay elders like to say, your path will open.[1]

Rule #1: Be fully engaged in the moment. The celebrated work of Jean Rouch has been seen, savored, and debated for more than seventy years. Scores of books have been written about Rouch in which scholars have discussed his use of the camera; his way of editing, which he called "fixing" the truth; his experience of *ciné-transe*, and his method of shared anthropology.[2] Rouch's films and his practices have had a profound impact on the history of visual anthropology and documentary filmmaking. Here I don't intend to survey a well-known and thoroughly discussed body of work; rather, I describe how the wisdom of the Songhay people profoundly shaped Rouch's approach to anthropology and to the world and how that approach can shape future work in anthropology.

I was drinking coffee in the dusty courtyard of the University of Niamey's Institute of Social Research. It was late December and I had just arrived from the United States to continue field research on Songhay spirit possession. A smiling Jean Rouch arrived and sat across from me.

"Paul, what are you doing today?"

I told him about my plans to visit several officials to finalize my research plans.

"They can wait, no?"

I shrugged.

"Drop your plans and come with me to *haro banda*"—beyond the water, or the Songhay way of saying the west bank of the River Niger. "I want you to see something over there."

I had learned that if Rouch asked you to go somewhere with him, it was always worth the effort of rearranging appointments. So we squeezed into his battered Citroën Deux Chevaux, crossed the John F. Kennedy bridge, and followed a circuitous network of dusty tracks into the heart of the haro banda neighborhood.

"You have to see this," Rouch said to me as we drove up to a thatch canopy, under which we found a gourd drummer and a monochord violinist. Rouch had brought me to the site of a soon-to-be-held spirit possession ceremony. Rouch bantered with the musicians and then giggled. They had apparently set up their instruments—and their ritual—opposite the villa of the rector of the Islamic University of Niamey. What better way to invoke the power of non-Islamic Songhay spirits in the face of a "foreign" force—Islam!

"Quite an act of political resistance, wouldn't you say?"

But our adventure was just beginning. Rouch told me to get into the car for another haro banda excursion.

"Where are we going?" I asked.

"You'll see."

We zigzagged along dusty paths until we parked in the courtyard of the Jane Rouch clinic, the domicile and workspace of Damouré Zika, a nurse who had been Rouch's collaborator for more than forty years. As we parked the car, Lam Ibrahim and Tallou Mouzourane, the other members of Rouch's gang, DELAROUTA, emerged and the merriment began. They told stories that made us laugh so hard that we fell to the ground.

"Ah," Damouré said, "this white man"—referring to me—"has learned to laugh with his body. It is through laughter, good feeling, and trust," he stated, "that we make our films. That's the way it's done."

So by following my path, no matter the circumstance, I stumbled upon the importance of humor and trust in anthropological fieldwork and film work, which led me to the second rule in the world according to Rouch.

Rule #2: Have confidence in your path and see where it and your imagination will take you. This rule helped me discover something new and wonderful in my work among West African street traders in New York City. One day Sidi Harouna, an African art trader, who looked like he was in his sixties, sat next to me and my friends at the Malcolm Shabazz market in Harlem. We got to talking and I soon discovered he was from Belayara, a town 100 kilometers northeast of Niger's capital, Niamey, and the site of a great market. He was tall, dressed in black shirt and black trousers. His face was square, his eyes cloudy, and his smile wide and broad.

"What are you doing here, Paul?" he asked.

"I'm doing my work here with my friends."

He slapped his leg and laughed. "You are wasting your time here."

My body stiffened with surprise.

"If you want to see a real market, come with me to Le Magasin [The Warehouse]."

"Le Magasin?"

"Let's go. Drop what you are doing and come with me."

Following rule #2 in the world according to Rouch, I dropped what I had been doing and followed this amiable stranger to Le Magasin, a seven-story warehouse packed with African art and African art traders—a place filled with wonder. In so doing, I stepped right into the next phase of my New York City fieldwork among West African traders. Surrounded by haunting statuettes, hand-woven blankets, camel saddles, and a varied assortment of tools and ornamental weapons, a new world of possibility presented itself.

During the filming of *Tourou et bitti* (1971), a gripping one-take film of spirit possession in Simiri, Niger, Rouch said that he had followed an uncertain path into the compound where dancing mediums had been struggling to attract spirits to their bodies. Putting his other project aside, he "let it roll" and filmed an extraordinary episode of spirit possession that inspired his notion of ciné-transe.

Rule #3: Open Your Ears and Listen Deeply to the Elders. The first two rules in the world according to Rouch are rather practical. They underscore the mindfulness of one's presence-in-the-field as well as the felicitous risk of seizing an opportunity—to interview or to film—and following that opportunity to wherever it leads. Rouch's third rule is more philosophical. In Songhay epistemology the young mind is undeveloped and not ready to take in truly powerful and potentially dangerous knowledge. Young apprentices must listen to their masters and watch them as they fish, weave, smith, play music, or mix healing potions. Opening one's ears means more than hearing what is said; it refers to the practice of deep listening, which is, in essence, listening to hear what someone is saying (see chapter 3). In practice, listening to a story compels you to pay attention to the interconnection of the senses as well as the connection between storytellers and their audiences.[3] Put another way, storytelling is a social activity that calls for sensework. Indeed, storytellers address their stories to all the senses, even taste, as in savoring the "sweetness" of a tale.[4]

It takes a long time for the elders to understand what is essential, what is important, and what is powerful. With the elders serving as guides, apprentices plunge into the classical knowledge of weaving, smithing, fishing, herbal medicine, sorcery, ethnography, and ethnographic film. They slowly build a foundation from which they can, through many trials and errors, gradually refine a set of practices. Eventually, they begin to practice what they have learned, and yet, their minds have not ripened enough to receive truly powerful knowledge. Through a long and slow trajectory of love and loss, they are eventually ready to receive from their masters the most important knowledge. Then and only then are they ready to fully practice their craft or science. Then and only then are they ready to fulfill their greatest obligation: to pass on their knowledge to the next generation of weavers, smiths, fishermen, herbalists, sorcerers, ethnographers, and ethnographic filmmakers.

Rouch learned from elder sorcerers in Niger and from the elders of the European film world. Through trial and error, he honed his filmmaking skills and demonstrated, following the Songhay way, a good measure of artistic playfulness and philosophic flexibility. As an elder he mentored ethnographic filmmakers in West Africa, Europe, and the United States—passing on his knowledge and practice to the next generation, all of which follows the principles of Songhay epistemology.

Rule #4: Open Yourself to the World and Let It Enter Your Being. The fourth rule in the world according to Rouch is profoundly existential. It requires an acceptance of vulnerability. Such vulnerability establishes and deepens human connection, which in turn enables the ethnographer or ethnographic filmmaker to experience social life more broadly and more meaningfully—to see and understand things that would be otherwise invisible or incomprehensible. In the introduction I quoted what the painter André Marchand said about the great Swiss artist Paul Klee, who opened his being to the worlds he wanted to paint. Such an opening is fraught with risk, not unlike the old man in the Sufi story recounted in the previous chapter. That man confronts his fear—his vulnerability—on a wind-whipped footbridge. Without taking the risk of making yourself existentially vulnerable, which is central to an artful ethnography, how can you proceed, how can you create, how can you make sense of the past and present, and how can you make your way toward the future?

From the earliest moments of Rouch's tenure in the Songhay world, he opened his being to the world of Songhay spirits and magic, following a path into a wondrous world that shaped his ethnographic and filmmaking practices. From the time that Damouré Zika's grandmother Kalia introduced Rouch to the spirit possession, Rouch followed the path of the spirits and did so for the rest of his long life. Rouch understood that if he wanted to film spirit possession ceremonies, which are the subject of many of his works, he would have to win the assent of the spirits. He realized that he had to demonstrate his respect for them. In time, the spirits came to know Rouch and would ask him to do things. Rouch told me that he regularly made sacrifices to Harakoy Dikko, goddess of the River Niger. He routinely sacrificed black goats to Dongo, the Songhay thunder god.

Rouch also had more subtle ways of demonstrating his fidelity and respect for Songhay spirits. He liked to wear baby blue socks and light blue shirts. These may have been his color of choice, and that tint of blue matched the color of his eyes, but that color also represented the spirit Nyalia, a cold spirit in the Songhay pantheon. Rouch's comportment, he often suggested to me, gave him access to the deep recesses of Songhay spirituality, which in turn enabled him to film ceremonies of great power and majesty.

Rule #5: Learn How to Tell a Good Story. In many respects, the first four rules cast a solid foundation for learning how to tell a good story, which, for Rouch and for me, is the most powerful representation of the ethnographic. In the world according to Rouch, story is primary. It connects the filmmaker or author to her or his audience. Theories come and go. Consider this very partial list of *classic* and *not-so-classic* anthropological theories that burned brightly at first, dimmed, and eventually faded away into the academic sunset: functionalism, structuralism, post-structuralism, ethno-science, ethnographic semantics, cultural materialism, the postmodern turn, the ontological turn, and post-humanism.

There is something about a story that has staying power. If an ethnographic story brings to life a setting and a cast of memorable characters, it can become a tale that is told and retold, read and re-read, and viewed and re-viewed. A good story inspires ongoing conversation and debate. Stories convey knowledge from generation to generation. Stories help us remember the dead. They enable us to grasp what is important in social life. In an essay about anthropological writing, Carole McGranahan wrote: "We tell stories to get to the point, to make our point. We miss that stories are the point. They are the getting and they are the there. . . . Anthropology is a storied discipline. This is one of our truths."[5]

In the formative years of Jean Rouch's ethnographic research and filmmaking in West Africa, he confronted a world in the throes of radical social change. Confronted with persistent racism, West Africans began to liberate themselves from the yoke of their colonial oppressors, which intensified tensions between colonizers (the French and British) and the colonized. How to make sense of such political, social, and cultural upheaval? Rouch chose the remedy of art, which compelled him to risk making films differently. Toward the end of the colonial epoch, Rouch invented a new film genre, ethno-fiction, that set the stage for his most original, enduring, and important films, *Les maîtres fous* (1955), *Moi, un noir* (1958), *La pyramide humaine* (1959), and *Chronique d'un été* (1960). Beset with multiple conflicts that have emerged from the social and political principles of petroculture, the world today is also in the throes of radical, political, and social change. How will we help shape a future that economic and political excess could imperil? In the final chapter of this book, I suggest that anthropologists seek the remedy of art to help secure a viable future.

7

Wisdom from the Edge of the Village

N'da ni ga gɛngi ngua, gengi ga ni ngua
"If you try to eat (consume) the bush, the bush will
eat (consume) you."

Adamu Jenitongo

It's not easy to live in Niger. The climate is hot and dry, which
means that Songhay people, most of whom are farmers, pay
particular attention to the weather. The dry season typically lasts
from October, the time of the millet harvest, until May, when the
first storms wet parched fields. The first rains of the season are usually few and far between—just enough moisture to plant seeds in
the fields. If it rains a few times in June and July, the millet stalks
emerge from sandy soil and begin to grow. The peak of the rainy
season is in August when it may rain five to ten times. During this
time the millet grows tall and sprouts seeds. In September it continues to rain but less often. The millet seeds are green—not yet
ripe. In October, also known as the little hot season, the hot sun
browns the millet seeds, which means they are ready for harvest.

This sequence of necessary climatic events is obviously delicate
—so much can easily go wrong. The rains can come late, which
delays planting. If it rains sufficiently in May, but there are no fur-
ther rains in June and July, the already planted millet seeds may

not germinate, or if they do, many of them will shrivel and die, which means that the August rains will not produce substantial millet growth. If all goes well, meaning that the right sequences of rain occur in May, June, July, and August and the millet matures, too much rain in September can rot stalks and seeds. Any deviation from the necessary sequence of rain events, then, can be catastrophic, resulting in a poor harvest of millet. Poor harvest years invariably mean widespread food shortages, famine, hunger, disease, and death.[1]

During one of my hot season fieldwork visits, a curious rainfall pattern developed. On five afternoons from mid-May to mid-June, dark clouds formed on Tillabéri's eastern horizon. A strong east wind whipped up, forming a looming cloud of dust. That same wind carried the smell of rain. In the normal scenario a thick suffocating wave of dust would slam into Tillabéri and eclipse the sun. From within the dust cloud, there would be thunder, which for Songhay people is the voice of the thunder god, Dongo. That sound signaled that rain would soon follow Dongo's path into Tillabéri and fall on the millet fields. The next day local farmers would be ready to plant.

When the expected storms approached Tillabéri that year, something curious occurred. The cloud would bifurcate, moving to the north and south, which meant that no rain fell on Tillabéri and its surrounding millet fields. Given the severity of the situation, town elders asked Adamu Jenitongo to stage a spirit possession ceremony. That ceremony took place on a sweltering Thursday afternoon—the principal day of the spirits.

Streams of musicians, praise singers, spirit mediums, town officials, and spectators flowed into Adamu Jenitongo's dune-top compound. Soon the violinist's one-stringed violin began to cry. Drummers struck clack-roll-clacks on their gourds. The sacred sounds echoed loudly in the hot air above Tillabéri, a signal for the spirits to swoop down from the sky and take the bodies of their mediums.

The seductive music compelled the impassioned dancing of old women. After the women had danced for close to one hour, my teacher, bone thin and spry in his frayed black tunic and baggy black drawstring trousers, walked up to the musicians.

"We need Hauka music. The Hauka can tell us what we need to know."

And so, the musicians began to play Hauka airs, hoping that the *old* sounds might entice the militaristic spirits of colonization to colonize a medium's body. In the searing heat of late afternoon, the musicians played and played. No Hauka came to claim the bodies of dancing mediums whose sweat-soaked clothing and sagging shoulders suggested their exhaustion. Finally, a Hauka came into the body of a young man, Daouda, himself a master of the one-stringed violin. His Hauka, Istambula, stomped in front of the musicians, saliva frothing from his mouth.

"I am Istambula," he announced. "I know why the rain is not coming to Tillabéri."

"Why is that?" Adamu Jenitongo asked the spirit.

"Someone blocked Dongo's path." Putting his arm on my mentor's shoulder, Istambula pointed to a car, a rusty Citroën Deux Chevaux that had been parked outside the compound's millet stalk fence. "You, me, and the *anasaara* [white man] will go into the bush." He pushed his finger into my chest. "Anasaara," he said, "you drive us into the bush. In the name of Bongi [God] the bush is dangerous. But we'll find the bad medicine."

The Citroën's owner overheard our conversation. He was a slight middle-aged man with a shaved head, wearing a loose gray shirt over a matching pair of trousers. Moussa approached me, Adamu Jenitongo, and the spirit, Istambula.

"I heard you," he said to Istambula. "You can use my car. I'll drive you into the bush."

Moussa then rolled back the car's canvas roof. Adamu Jenitongo and I squeezed into the narrow back seat. Istambula, still frothing saliva and bellowing about treachery in Tillabéri, got in next to Moussa and stood up in the roofless car. He pointed to a path that led to the east. "I'll show you where to go."

We followed tracks that took us across a barren laterite plain. When we attempted to cross a wadi, the tires got stuck in deep sand. Moussa, who was used to the difficulties of driving in the bush, put some metal tracks under the rear tires, which, when we pushed forward, dislodged the Deux Chevaux. Liberated, we drove down an embankment toward a patch of green that marked a water hole. A sandstone butte with jagged streaks of red and orange rose in the golden light of late afternoon. As the pond's water came into view, Istambula shook violently and used his fists to pound the edge of the windshield. With his forefinger, he pointed to a tall termite hill.

"Stop," he ordered. "Stop."

He bounded out of the car and strutted toward the termite hill.

"Look here," he said. "Look here."

We all got out and inspected the termite hill. Istambula fell to his knees. Using his fingernails, he scraped at the hill's mud-baked base. He stood up, pounded his chest, and bellowed. "Here it is. Here it is."

At the base of the termite hill, we noticed the roundish opening of a buried antelope horn. Moussa found a sharp-edged stick and began to scrape the sun-baked mud around the horn. In time Adamu Jenitongo extracted it from the hill. When he shook the horn, several amulets that had been stuffed inside fell to the ground.

FIGURE 10
A West African termite hill. © Paul Stoller.

"Very bad medicine," Tillabéri's sohanci said. "Someone wanted to spoil the rain. We have to fix it."

The sohanci asked us to find some kindling to build a fire. When the fire got hot, he asked the bush for forgiveness. He then threw the antelope horn and the amulets into the fire, which, he said, would kill the spell.

We returned to Moussa's car—three men and one spirit, who continued to speak in tongues, froth at the mouth, and complain about deteriorating social conditions in Tillabéri.

Istambula pointed toward the west. "We must leave the bush before nightfall. The bush is dangerous at night."

When Istambula sat down in the front passenger seat, the spirit slipped out of its medium, Daouda. Losing consciousness, Daouda slumped in his seat.

Adamu Jenitongo leaned forward and shook Daouda, which revived him. He coughed several times and asked for water, which I gave to him from my canteen.

The sohanci pointed his forefinger skyward and said: "With the help of the spirits, we found bad medicine, which they put on Dongo's path."

"Why?" I asked.

"I don't know," my teacher replied, "but that bad medicine did move the rain to the north and south." Adamu Jenitongo looked back at the termite hill. "We'll have to make offerings to the spirits of the bush to set things right."

For four days, the sohanci recited incantations to restore harmony between village and bush. For the first three days he sacrificed chickens. On the fourth day, he sacrificed a black goat—which is Dongo's familiar.

Five days later rain came to Tillabéri.

Six days later the villagers trekked to their fields and planted millet.

That year the harvest was a good one.

After the incident of bad rain medicine, Songhay people in Tillabéri continued to pay attention to the sky, the wind, and the dust. For them such attention has always been a matter of life and death. The years flowed by. Sometimes Tillabéri friends sent news of a good harvest. I would often receive news of a drought that had decimated the millet crop. Some years I would receive news of catastrophic floods that rotted the millet and washed away many mud-brick homes. Many years brought news of disease and death.

After a long hiatus, I returned to West Africa in 2010 to see several Nigerien friends I had met in Harlem's Malcolm Shabazz market, a sensuous slice of West African social life in one of the Big Apple's most fabled neighborhoods. As soon as I landed in Niamey, Niger's capital city, the oven-hot heat of the Nigerien afternoon took hold of my body. The airport hadn't changed that much, but I immediately noticed something I had never witnessed in Niger—a serious traffic jam. The smell of car exhaust permeated the stale air. Blaring car horns disturbed what used to be the quiet peace of a late Sahelian afternoon.

I found a taxi and in short order the driver deposited me at the research center of the University of Niamey where I had reserved a modest room—whitewashed walls, a floor of cracked ceramic tiles, an anemic ceiling fan, a tired air conditioner, a single bed with a thin mattress, two sheets, a well-used pillow, a shower, and a bathroom with a dingy sink, a chipped mirror, two threadbare towels, and a functioning toilet. In search of street food for dinner, I left my room. Before I reached the street, however, the Research Center's guard invited me to his home, a whitewashed, two-room, tin-roofed cement structure. We feasted on meat, savory sauce, rice, and lots of good talk.

The next morning I walked up a dusty dirt road to the Le Petit Marché, a place where I spent many wonderful hours sitting on tree-shaded straw mats, talking with herbalists as they prescribed medicine for skin ulcers, lung congestion, malaria, and dysentery. After such a long absence I was delighted to find one of my herbalist friends. Most of the others, he told me, had relocated to the countryside.

From Le Petit Marché, I trudged to the main market, Le Grand Marché. The city seemed dirtier, more congested. Skeletal beggars asked me for a few coins so they might get something to eat. Toward midday, I heard the call to prayer and saw hundreds of the faithful block Niamey's main street as they pledged their fidelity to Allah.

Once in the market, I asked people where I might find El Hajj Angu's stall. In anticipation of once again seeing my friend, I began my search through the market's narrow passageways.

Years before, I met Angu Sandi during fieldwork among West African immigrants in New York City.[2] After the devaluation of the West African franc (CFA) had reduced the value of his holdings by 50 percent, Angu Sandi took what was left in the bank and bought an airplane ticket to New York City. Tapping into a network of West African traders in Harlem, he set up a table on the sidewalk of 125th Street, near the marquis of the famed Apollo Theater, where he sold baseball caps, gloves, perfumes, soap, and body oils. After a year in Harlem, he and a friend, Mounkaila, moved to Greensboro, North Carolina, where Angu worked as a forklift operator at a textile factory and a dishwasher at a Radisson hotel. Sharing sleeping quarters with compatriots, he worked for several years saving as much money as he could.

Once he had sufficient investment funds, he and Mounkaila returned to Niger to start a car business. At first, they would fly to Germany, buy a Mercedes, drive the luxury car from Europe, cross the Sahara, and end up in Niger, where they'd sell it for a profit. Eventually, they figured out that the costs (incidents of banditry, engine failure, and bribes to customs officials) far outweighed the benefits, and Angu set up a network of people to facilitate international car trading. He would travel to car auctions in places like

Richmond, Virginia, or Harrisburg, Pennsylvania, get a broker to purchase two or three cars, then transport the cars to a detailer in port cities like Baltimore, Maryland, Charleston, South Carolina, or Jacksonville, Florida. Once detailed, the cars, mostly Toyotas and Hondas, would be sent via reasonably priced cargo ships to Cotonou, Benin, where they would be sold and sent up-country to their destination. The car business made Angu a wealthy merchant, enabling him to undertake the expensive pilgrimage to Mecca. He also used his wealth to support his family and provide food and medicine for the more destitute people of his Niamey neighborhood.

When I showed up at his market stall, El Hajj Angu was on the phone with one of his trading partners in Frankfurt, Germany. When he got off, he said:

"Let's go to lunch. I know a good rice and sauce place not too far from here. We'll take my car."

The street food was excellent, but because he was incessantly on the phone forging deals in Dubai, Bamako, Mali, and Beijing, it was difficult for us to have a conversation. After completing a call with his son, who oversaw his operations in Jacksonville, Florida, we finally had some time to reflect on the state of the world. I mentioned that Niger had changed a great deal in a relatively short period of time.

"Yes," he said. "It is different because of drought. The rains no longer come when they're supposed to, and people can't grow enough food to feed their families."

"And what about the countryside?"

"No rain, no crops, no food."

"And people have to leave?"

"That's why I went to America. There was no food here, and commerce was bad, so I went to America. That's why so many people have come to Niamey. It's too crowded. There isn't enough rain. Young people don't want to farm. There's not enough water. There's filth and garbage everywhere. More old people are hungry. More children die. People have always been poor here, but now it's worse. The rainy season is different now. Look at how it has changed everything."

"We have some of these problems in America," I said. "There's more and more poverty."

"There is no longer any harmony in the world."

"What can be done?" I asked.

"Our leaders don't care. Does Obama care?" he wondered.

"I think he does, but it's not enough, is it?"

He nods his head. "Perhaps our future is in the hands of Allah."

"My teacher, Adamu Jenitongo," I told him, "liked to say that we need to pay more attention to the bush. We need to respect its power."

"That's the hard truth," El Hajj Angu stated. "The elders understand how the world works. We need to listen to them and follow their advice."

I felt a heavy sadness as I realized, perhaps for the first time, how much climate change—the result of human behavior in the world—had degraded the quality of social life in Niger.

Such degradation, of course, is not limited to countries like Niger. Consider the plight of the Yanomamo people whose federally protected lands in Brazil have been the site of recent killings. The activities of unlicensed gold miners have polluted the rivers. Their presence has also infected and/or killed many Yanomami. Recently, armed miners drove their speedboats along Yanomamo rivers, shooting indiscriminately at people—men, women, and children—in riverain villages.[3] Here is what one Yanomamo shaman, Davi Kopenawa, had to say about the Western attempts to master the bush and the dangerous conditions the culture of mastery creates for his people in contemporary Brazil.

> When they speak about the forest, white people often use the word "environment." What they refer to in this way is what remains of everything they have destroyed so far. I don't like this word. The Earth cannot be split apart as if the forest were just a leftover part. With leftover trees and leftover rivers, leftover game, fish and humans who live there, its breath of life will become too short. That is why we are worried. We shamans simply say we are protecting nature as a whole thing. We defend the forests' trees, mountains and rivers, its fish, game, spirits, and human inhabitants. We even defend the land of the white people beyond it and all who live there.[4]

In both the Songhay and Yanomamo cases, people believe strongly that contemporary ecological adversities—droughts, floods, pollution—result from human activities like subverting the rain in Tillabéri or gold mining that triggers pollution and violence in Brazil.

The human origin of climate devastation can also be linked to Hurricane Dorian, the 2020 storm that devastated the Bahamas. In 2021 Bahamians continued to suffer. In a *New York Times* column Bahamian poet and essayist Bernard Ferguson bore witness to the power of nature, or, as Songhay people would say, the power of the bush.

> This May—20 months after Hurricane Dorian unleashed its cruelty upon my Bahamas—I looked down from an airplane's window and could see land that was still visibly wounded. Grand Bahama and the Abacos were once covered in dark green foliage that complemented the emerald waters; now long stretches had faded to brown, even gray. Two-story waves had blown apart wide sections of shoreline. Once-gorgeous mangrove swamps—habitat for algae and crabs and bonefish, and the land's defense against a

storm's surge—were overwhelmed by Dorian's salt water, and large swaths of them lay dead, their brittle shells shimmering in the heat. The same fate befell the abundant indigenous Caribbean pine trees, which take decades to grow to their towering heights of over 100 feet. They need fresh water to survive, so when the ocean stretched upon the land and sat there for days, it killed acres of them.[5]

Long before Ferguson's people settled in the Bahamas, the Taino farmed the fertile island lands. Like the Songhay and Yanomamo, the Taino harbored a deep respect for the power of nature, the power of the bush. "Before my mother, before Bahamians, before the colonizers and the enslaved people they dragged here," Ferguson wrote in his *New York Times* piece,

> it was in large part the Indigenous Taíno who cultivated the lands. They believed hurricanes arrived because of the powers of the zemis, or divine deities. The Taíno feared and respected these zemis, whose powers often devastated Taíno communities. To survive, they sheltered in sturdy structures when storms came, praying to be spared. European colonizers, before killing nearly all the Taíno, took note of these strategies—knowledge passed down across the time of colonization that serves as a basis for Bahamians today.[6]

Like the Songhay and the Yanomamo, the Taino believed that hurricanes emerged from the displeasure of divine deities who had been disrespected through thoughtless human activity. From a Bahamian perspective, Ferguson suggests, increasingly powerful hurricanes are the

> consequence of decisions made by wealthy nations beyond our shores, and the greenhouse gas emissions that have fueled their prosperity and way of life. Most of these gases have come from the United States, China, the European Union, Russia, and other developed countries. Compared with them, the Bahamas' own emissions are tiny. And yet it is the Bahamas, along with other small islands

worldwide—like Antigua and Barbuda, the Maldives, Kiribati and the Marshall Islands—that are on the front lines of the climate crisis.[7]

The ramifications of human-produced climate change have also had negative impacts on indigenous peoples in North America. In their 2021 *New York Times* story, Flavelle and Goodluck reported on the climatic plight of Native Americans. They wrote:

> From Alaska to Florida, Native Americans are facing severe climate challenges, the newest threat in a history marked by centuries of distress and dislocation. While other communities struggle on a warming planet, Native tribes are experiencing an environmental peril exacerbated by policies—first imposed by white settlers and later the United States government—that forced them onto the country's least desirable lands.
>
> And now, climate change is quickly making that marginal land uninhabitable. The first Americans face the loss of home once again. In the Pacific Northwest, coastal erosion and storms are eating away at tribal land, forcing native communities to try to move inland. In the Southwest, severe drought means the Navajo Nation is running out of drinking water. At the edge of the Ozarks, heirloom crops are becoming harder to grow, threatening to disconnect the Cherokee from their heritage.[8]

So once again the decisions of others have accelerated the climate crisis—rising seas, melting permafrost, severe drought, and wildfires. These devastating developments threaten the social, cultural, and political existence of indigenous people in North America. They threaten to undermine the relationship of people to place, an important and central tenet to groups like the Songhay, Yanomamo, Bahamians, and Native Americans. In his classic work, *Wisdom Sits in Places*, Keith Basso considered this central principal. He wrote that places possess a marked capacity for triggering acts of self-reflection, inspiring thoughts about who one presently is, or memories of who one used to be, or musings on who one might become. And that is not all. Place-based thoughts about the self lead commonly to thoughts of other things—other places, other people, other times, whole networks of associations that ramify unaccountably within the expanding spheres of awareness that they themselves engender. The experience of sensing places, then, is thus both roundly reciprocal and incorrigibly dynamic. As places animate the ideas and feelings of persons who attend to them, these same ideas and feelings animate the places on which attention has been bestowed, and the movements of this process—inward toward facets of the self, outward toward aspects of the external world, alternately both together—cannot be known in advance. When places are actively sensed, the physical landscape becomes wedded to the landscape of the mind, to the roving imagination, and where the mind may lead is anybody's guess.[9]

Basso goes on to quote a Western Apache elder, Dudley Patterson, who spoke philosophically about the importance of space and place—the bush—for indigenous people. Dudley Patterson says:

Wisdom sits in places. It's like water that never dries up. You need to drink water to stay alive, don't you? Well, you also need to drink from places. You must remember everything about them. You must learn their names. You must remember what happened at them long ago. You must think about it and keep on thinking about it. Then your mind will become smoother and smoother. Then you will see danger before it happens. You will walk a long way and live a long time. You will be wise. People will respect you.[10]

For many peoples in the world, soil, wind, clouds, trees, and water—all elements of what West Africans call the bush—are intrinsic to their being-in-the-world. Songhay elders like Adamu Jenitongo liked to tell me that to live well in the world, people must respect the bush (see chapter 5). If human beings disrespect the bush, the bush unleashes it fury.

That fury has become increasingly evident in the non-indigenous world. In 2005 Hurricane Katrina caused more than 1,800 deaths and $125 billion in property damages in Louisiana.[11] In 2012 Hurricane Sandy ravaged the New Jersey and New York coastlines, resulting in 233 deaths and $70 billion in property damage.[12] In 2020 drought conditions in California fueled a horrific wildfire season. In that year 9,917 fires burned 4,397,809 acres of forest. The gigafire of August 2020 burned nearly one million acres in seven counties, destroying ten thousand structures, resulting in more than $10 billion in property damage.[13] As I suggested in the prelude of this book, when the temperature in Portland, Oregon, soars to 115 degrees, it might be time to begin listening to the wise words of people like Adamu Jenitongo, Davi Kopenawa, and Dudley Patterson.

I recently participated in a virtual seminar in which anthropologists and philosophers present works in progress. The theme of the seminar was the notion of looming. The presenter, Jason Throop, discussed his experiences at the beginning of the COVID-19 epidemic. In the essay he eloquently discussed the impact that the looming presence of COVID-19 had for himself and his family.[14] Using various philosophical perspectives, the participants tried to define the indeterminate fuzziness of "looming." For me, "looming" conjures an image of a gathering wave of dust that is slowly but inexorably coming to engulf me in a hundred-foot choking cloud, a cloud that eclipses the sun.

The COVID-19 pandemic is like a dust storm that has engulfed all of us. It is choking our future. We find ourselves today in a perilously stressful state. COVID-19 is everywhere and is going nowhere. Despite the increasingly rapid rate of highly effective vaccinations and treatments, there are ever-emerging and more contagious variants of the virus that are spreading widely in Europe, North America, Asia, South America, and Africa.

Indeed, in the United States COVID-19 fatigue has become the new norm. Tired of social-distancing protocols, millions of unvaccinated people have been taking risks that not only endanger themselves and their loved ones but also the complete strangers they might encounter at a restaurant, a grocery store, an airport, or a social event. What's more, the poor peoples of the world have been victims of vaccine apartheid. In Africa, for example, the emerging variants of COVID-19 spread rapidly across the continent. In Mali, for example, only 1.9 percent of the population is fully vaccinated.[15] In short, the coronavirus is not likely to disappear. And who is to say that COVID-19 is a singular phenomenon? Given the ongoing degradation of the natural world, we can probably expect another virus to jump from the bush, as people say in West Africa, to the village. As the highly respected Ali Khan, the former director of the CDC's Office of Public Health and Preparedness, wrote, "the virus will quietly spread from rat to rat or squirrel to squirrel, year after year out in the jungle, and you'll never know it except for the sporadic human infection. Then suddenly, out of the blue, you've got a new human epidemic on your hands."[16]

But the stressful realities of COVID-19's robustness are only part of the picture. There is troublesome turmoil in the world. In western Niger, as I mentioned at the beginning of this book, Islamists routinely loot small villages and demand protection tribute from farmers who, if they're lucky, earn $300 a year. If the peasant farmers don't comply, the Islamists kill them. What had been a poor place graced with gracious conviviality and beautiful ceremony is now beset with religious intolerance and the violence of hate.

Sadly, these trends are widespread. In the United States there has been no shortage of systematic racism, ethnic discrimination, hateful violence, income inequality, and, of course, coronavirus infections, hospitalizations, and deaths—all of which create ever-present anxiety and stress—especially if you are neither white nor Christian. If you combine these elements, which are inextricably linked, we are all standing in the path of a looming wave of dust about to overwhelm us. In such moments of terror, we are immobilized. Our lives flash before our eyes. What must we know to confront the looming storm?

How did we get to this precarious state?

Many scholars believe our contemporary state of emergency can be traced to the long-standing culture of extraction, the fundamental tenet of which is that human beings can dominate nature and one another.[17] Since the Industrial Revolution human beings have extracted from nature fossil fuels, minerals, trees, and water. In doing so we have depleted the earth's natural resources and produced polluting agents that have brought on the death of forests as well as the plastic and mineral degradation of rivers, oceans, coral reefs, and landscapes—all in the name of progress and capitalism. Since the Industrial Revolution states and/or individuals have expanded the will to power to sustain regimes of social and political dominance.[18] These have brought us warfare, famine, misery, social inequality, racism, and the violence of hate. Even in the sciences and social sciences we are compelled to extract principles, formulas, categories, definitions, and theories from the free flow of experience, all of which give us a sense of control and certainty. We study. We know. We understand—or think we understand.

In their revolutionary and insightful book, *Hyposubjects: On Becoming Human*, Morton and Boyer wrote:

> mastery, transcendence, excess—that is the world that we know. Those are the qualities of this era. And with the refinement of excessive mastery in various localities has emerged relentless predatory impulses—monotheistic, capitalistic—to bring the world into alignment with our transcendence mission. An imploded form of subjectivity is worth considering as an antidote. One that is denser, but also, more aware of the architecture of its density and of the gravitational forces that hold it together, one that is not constantly seeking the beyond.[19]

For me one antidote to pervasive extractive mastery is the rediscovery and recognition of indigenous wisdom. People like the Songhay of Niger, the Yanomamo of Brazil, and the Western Apache of New Mexico and Arizona understand well the relationship of bush to village. The bush is always more powerful and dangerous than the village. If the forces of the bush are not respected, those forces bring drought, floods, destruction, diseases like COVID-19, and death. If you attempt to consume the bush, it will ultimately consume you. For Songhay people who live in harm's way day in and day out, there is little control and no certainty. They accept their existential limits and live fully within them, which, in the end, enables them to live robustly in profoundly challenging physical, economic, and political circumstances.[20] Like other indigenous populations, Songhay people like Adamu Jenitongo understand that to avoid wholesale extinction—the bush totally consuming the village—much change is needed—more modesty, creativity, flexibility, and playfulness, and less certainty, mastery, and domination.

So what does listening to people like Adamu Jenitongo or Davi Kopenawa entail?

First and foremost, it entails a project of unlearning, which, in turn, requires the modest admission of not-knowing. It also necessitates the recognition that the power of the bush is always already present, a power, as the COVID-19 pandemic has demonstrated, over which human beings have limited control. Morton and Boyer have much to suggest about this species-saving course of action. Given the power of their prose, I quote them at length.

> We live in a time of hyperobjects, of objects too massive and multiphasic in their distribution in time and space for humans to fully comprehend or experience them in a unitary way. A black hole is a kind of hyperobject, a biosphere is another. But many of the hyperobjects that concern us have human origins. For example, global warming. Or antibiotics. Or plastic bags. Or capitalism. These hyperobjects exceed and envelop us like a viscous fog, they make awkward and unexpected appearances, they inspire hypocrisy and lameness and dread. A certain kind of human has helped usher the world into the hyperobjective era. Let's call them hypersubjects. You will recognize them as the type of subjects you are invited to vote for in elections, the experts who tell you how things are, the people shooting in your schools, the mansplainers from your Twitter feed. Hypersubjects are typically but not exclusively white, male, northern, well-nourished, modern in all senses of the term. They wield reason and technology, whether cynically or sincerely, as instruments for getting things done. They command and control, they seek transcendence, they get very high on their own supply of dominion.[21]

In the end Morton and Boyer suggest:

> In sum, for the moment, the transcendent hypersubject continues to stalk the earth. But he is doing so in an increasingly flickering,

even spectral way; his monophasic being is perpetually out of sync. Half aware that his time is past, he lashes out violently, pouts, negates any alternative, bargains for salvational machines and afterlife redemptions. You might pity him had he not left so much ruin and despair in his wake. . . . But as in Alfonso Cuarón's film *Gravity*, what awaits us instead is fabricating a future out of ruins and preparing for a long perilous voyage back to earth. That future will belong to hyposubjects; if we wish to thrive, we will become human again as hyposubjects.[22]

Using different languages and different cultural references and echoing the old words of their ancestors, people like Adamu Jenitongo, Davi Kopenawa, and Dudley Patterson wonder if we will become human again.

What is the alternative?

Coda

In this book I have attempted to show how anthropological insights about the human condition are important elements in any future blueprint for social and cultural change. It is no exaggeration to state that the world is in trouble. As I suggested in the previous chapter, our routine social, cultural, political, and ecological expectations have been undermined.[1] In the July–August 2021 edition of *Anthropology News*, five political anthropologists offered a collaborative manifesto for doing anthropology in an admittedly turbulent world. They wrote passionately and intelligently about the need for present and future anthropologists to be more collaborative and more politically engaged. They mentioned the need to expand our research methodologies and recalibrate our disciplinary priorities. In a time of crisis, their manifesto was a multifaceted call to action. One of the contributors, David Vine, wrote: "The COVID-19 pandemic, the global economic crisis, the unprecedented uprisings for justice have demonstrated the urgency of dedicating our skills, anthropological or otherwise, to healing the world."[2]

It is important that anthropologists read and act on the insightful thoughts expressed in the collaborative manifesto. In articulating his thoughts about doing anthropology in a turbulent world, David Gellner, another contributor to the collaborative manifesto, wrote convincingly about the need for more collaborative research efforts.

"Accomplishing multisited, multiscaled ethnographies requires," he stated, "teams of researchers with at least partially shared agendas, followed by collaborative—and doubtless painful—writing up."[3] In *Wisdom from the Edge* I have tried to add another dimension for doing anthropology in a turbulent world: the use of analytically informed sensuous narrative to compel readers to turn the page. Indeed, writing accessible and compelling prose usually involves more than *writing up* the results of research. The subtext of this book is that anthropologists can produce rigorously researched narrative works that are attuned to an age of crises. Those works, in turn, can connect to a broad audience of people the profoundly important anthropological insights mentioned in the manifesto. Accordingly, artful ethnographic writing is a powerful way to extend much-needed indigenous knowledge to a world in dire need of indigenous wisdom.

Sensuous storytelling that evokes space and place, hones in on the sonority of vibrant dialogue, and depicts the idiosyncrasies of character can create works in which indigenous wisdom jumps from the author's page to the reader's mind. The collaborative manifesto calls for revamped anthropological telling, which is vital to our disciplinary future. Telling, after all, is a necessary condition in any design for (disciplinary) change. But is there not more disciplinary space for *showing*—more evocation in artful storytelling? Through empirically informed sensuous storytelling, *showing* can be combined with *telling* to powerfully communicate important anthropological insights to the public. In short, a more intense focus on writing-as-art can ensure that our slowly developed insights can become fundamental elements in the public sphere, elements that contribute directly to healing a world confronting a set of life-threatening social, cultural, ecological, and political crises.

It had been a typically hot day in Adamu Jenitongo's Tillabéri compound—too hot to do anything in the afternoon except lay on palm frond mats in the shade of the compound's stick-and-thatch hangar, drink warm water, sip on sweet Chinese tea, swat flies, and talk about the past and present in Tillabéri. The sohanci smiled as he reminisced about unblocking Dongo's path earlier that month.

"Since then," he said, "the rains have been just right—not too much, not too little. We'll make sure to continue our offerings and with the help of the king of sky [Dongo], we'll have a good harvest in October."

"Iri koy ma ta," said Moru Adamu, my mentor's short, stocky, and round-faced youngest son. The haze of the afternoon heat dulled his large brown eyes, which were set far apart on his round face.

"I hope the offerings are accepted," I said.

"If our hearts are pure, the offerings will be accepted," Adamu Jenitongo said.

FIGURE 11
Adamu Jenitongo weaving grass rope in his Tillabéri compound. © Paul Stoller.

To pass the time in the hazy heat, the sohanci braided dried grasses into rope. Moru dozed. Hoping for a soothing breeze, I read a novel. Eventually, I too dozed off. The sound of men greeting one another aroused me from my heat-induced stupor. My teacher had left the hangar's shade to greet his guests. I nudged Moru, who slowly opened his eyes.

"What's going on?" I asked.

"Those men are all sohanci from the region. Every so often they come here to meet and talk."

It was like a sorcerer's convention, I thought to myself, at the edge of the village. "Can I go over there and introduce myself?"

Moru chuckled. "They know who you are." Moru pushed himself to his feet and dusted off his trousers. "Let's go over there."

The men had gathered in the shade of a jujube tree. Palm frond mats had been unrolled. A soft breeze carried the aroma of steeping tea. Kola nuts had been piled in a small gourd situated in the middle of the assorted mats. A large gourd had been filled with water. A wooden ladle had been placed next to the gourd. In the distance we could hear the rhythmic thumps of pestles striking mortars to produce millet flour—late afternoon preparations for the evening meal.

Like Adamu Jenitongo, all but one of the men wore black tunics, black drawstring trousers, and black turbans. They grunted as they lowered their old bodies to the mats and tried to find a comfortable position on their pillows. Unlike the others, one man wore a long white boubou over white drawstring trousers. A red fez covered his head. He sat down on a metal chair. One of my teacher's grandsons brought him a small bowl of water. He sipped the water and then spoke to the group.

"My friends, we are all the children of our fathers and our father's fathers. How good it is to meet here in Tillabéri!"

The other men voiced their affirmations.

"We may all be old, moving toward the end of our paths, but we still have much to learn, do we not?"

Another chorus of affirmations.

The seated man went on to talk about the sacred obligation of elders—to continue to learn and to pass their knowledge on to the next generation. He talked about his father and his grandfather and how his people had migrated from Wanzerbe, the center of sohanci power, to Ouallam—hundreds of kilometers east of Tillabéri.

Not daring to sit among such a powerful and august group of sohanci elders, Moru and I stood at the edge of the gathering.

"Who is that man in the chair?" I whispered to Moru.

"He's Djingarey Niandou," Moru said. "He's the great sorcerer of Ouallam." Moru pinched my arm. "He's even older than my father."

I silently calculated that Djingarey Niandou would be more than a hundred years old. As the oldest and most distinguished practitioner among these healers, it was fitting that he sat in a chair symbolically *above* the other sorcerers.

One of the men gave the oldest sorcerer a kola nut. He opened the nut and began to chew on a piece of it. He pointed to one of the old men on the mat. "Ousmane, tell us what you've been doing."

Using his elbow, Ousmane propped himself up on his pillow. "My father," he said to the older man, "I recently used the plant *wata gaya gaya* on a woman with stomach pains."

"Did it work?" the older healer asked.

"It worked very fast—no problems. It's the first time I used it for the stomach."

"I've not used it for stomach pain," Adamu Jenitongo chimed in, "but I have great respect for our brother's knowledge of plants. I'll start using it here in Tillabéri."

The other practitioners all reported on their latest experiments. For several hours they shared recipes for potions and discussed the prescription for a particular plant leaf harvested in daylight as opposed to one harvested at night. They shared information on the various uses of plant roots as opposed to plant stems or leaves. They had impassioned debates about the bush. In the bush, they agreed, the spirits are powerful, a place frequented by human as well as spirit enemies. Each practitioner spoke of an increasing lack of respect for the old ways and the old words they had long ago committed to memory.

"Look what the lack of respect has brought us," Djingarey Niandou stated. "We have either too little or too much rain. There's not enough food for our families. Children are hungry. People are sick. You can smell death in the air."

"Niger is a hard country," Adamu Jenitongo said. "We bring this misery upon ourselves. We have lost respect for the bush."

Clicking their tongues against their palates, the men vocalized their agreement.

"As elders it is our obligation," Djingarey Niandou said, "to respect the forces of the bush so that we maintain harmony in the village. Yes, we are strong people, but the bush is stronger than we are. We must respect its power. We must continue to teach our people to live in harmony with it. If we try to master the bush, the bush will master us."

With that proclamation Djingarey Niandou stood up, signaling the end of the gathering. He shook Adamu Jenitongo's hand and expressed his gratitude for the latter's hospitality.

"It has been a good day," Adamu Jenitongo said.

"May the bush take notice of our fidelity to the old ways," Djingarey Niandou said as he moved toward the entrance to Adamu Jenitongo's compound.

We returned to the hangar, where we would soon share an evening meal of millet paste smothered with baobab leaf sauce.

"This has been a good day," the sohanci said to me. "You've walked in the bush. You've witnessed its power. Today you learned why we must respect its power."

Thinking back to that remarkable edge-of-the-village gathering of the region's senior sorcerers, I began to understand more clearly the importance of the bush. Adamu Jenitongo tapped the bush not only to generate his sorcerous power but to refine his thinking. During his long life he attempted to reconfigure the balance between women and men, between haves and have-nots, between culture and nature, and between village and bush. That harmony can not only ensure the viability of the village but secure the future of the world.

Such is the wisdom from the edge of the village.

Notes

Introduction

1. Merleau-Ponty 1964. Merleau-Ponty's *Eye and Mind* is a more focused aspect of his broader project in the phenomenology of perception and intersubjectivity. Like almost all of his works, it is a wonderfully poetic exploration of the sensuous contours of the social life.

2. Jackson 2016a.

3. Merleau-Ponty 1964, 22.

4. Merleau-Ponty 1964, 16.

5. Charbonnier 1959, cited in Merleau-Ponty 1964, 31.

6. Nietzsche [1876] 1956, 93.

7. Merleau-Ponty 1964, 139.

8. Merleau-Ponty 1969, 20.

9. See Waterston and Cordon's *Light in Dark Times* (2020) for an example of artful ethnography, a text that blends image and text into a moving, widely accessible work on the state of the human condition in contemporary times. See also Waterston 2013. Other examples, among many, include Catherine Trundle's *Americans in Tuscany* (2014), S. Locklann Jain's *Things That Art* (2019), Piers Vitebsky's *The Reindeer People* (2005), and Sherine Hamdy and Coleman Nye's *Lissa: A Story about Medical Promise, Friendship and Revolution* (2017).

10. Jackson 2016a.

11. Derrida 1984, 117.

12. Jackson 2016a, 50.

13. See Derrida 1984; Jackson 2016a, 50.

14. Jackson 2016a, 204.

15. Dewey 1929.

16. See Jackson 2016b; Durkheim 1912.

17. Jackson 2016a, 204.

18. Agee and Evans 1941, 365.
19. Narayan 1989, 1.
20. Badkhen 2018, 1–2.
21. Faye 2018, 64.
22. Bessire 2021, 1.
23. See Geertz 1988.
24. Author's files.
25. Mosley 2005, 87–88.
26. Hammer 2016, 50–51.
27. Behar 1996, 45–46.
28. Hurston 1935, 7–8.
29. Chabon 1995, 7–8.
30. Badkhen 2016, 49–50.
31. Ulysse 2017, 98.
32. See Stoller 2020a.
33. Bruner 1991.
34. Gottschall 2012, 138.
35. For more on art, ethnography, and the senses, see Cox, Irving, and Wright 2016; Schneider 2016. For a comprehensive overview of sensorial studies, see David Howes's *The Sensory Studies Manifesto: Tracking the Sensorial Revolution in the Arts and the Human Sciences* (2022).

1. Imaging Knowledge

1. See Taylor 2014; Turkle 2016.
2. See Henley 2009; Feld 2003; Predal 1982.
3. Holtedahl 1995.
4. Holtedahl 2018.
5. Holtedahl 2018, liner notes.
6. Martinez 1992, 132.
7. Rouch 1952.
8. See Henley 2009. This work is simply the best critical appreciation of Jean Rouch's work, especially the section on Rouch's editing practices, which he called "fixing the truth."
9. Arntsen and Holtedahl 2005, 69.
10. See Rouch 1955, 1958, 1959, 1960.
11. Pratt 1986.
12. See Riesman 1977, a classic work on Fulani codes of behavior in Burkina Faso.
13. Buber 1971.
14. See Petrini 1987 and Berg and Seeber 2016 on the slow movement in academia.
15. See Eliot 1968.

2. In the Shade of the Jujube Tree

1. See Shack and Skinner 1979 and Whitehouse 2012, among many titles on strangers in African societies.

2. Stoller 2017.

3. Stoller and Olkes 1987.

4. See Stoller 2014; Stoller and Olkes 1987.

5. See Griaule and Dieterlen 1969.

6. See Bascombe 1969; Devisch 1985; Holbrand 2012; Peek 1991; Werbner 2015; and Zempleni 1968, among many titles on divination in Africa and divinatory practices in the New World.

7. Arendt 1958.

8. See Chernoff 1979; Downey 2005; Friedson 1996; Wacquant 2004; Stoller and Olkes 1987; Landry 2019; Stoller 2008.

9. See Martínez, Di Puppo, and Frederiksen 2021.

3. Sensory Dimensions of Spirit Possession

1. See Stoller 1992; Henley 2009.

2. See Bastide 1978.

3. See Tylor 1871; Frasier 1890.

4. See Harris 1957 for an astute and sensitive analysis of possession as "hysteria."

5. See Lewis 1971; Bourguignon 1976; and Goodman 1990, to cite only a few.

6. See Harris 1957; Monfouga-Nicholas 1972; and Zempleni 1968 for African examples; see also Obeysekere 1981 and Crapanzano 1980 for exceptional works in this tradition.

7. See Pidoux 1955; A. Jackson 1968; Sturtevant 1968; Gell 1980; Kehoe and Giletti 1980.

8. See Balandier 1980; Lambek 1981; Boddy 1989.

9. Stoller 1997, 19–20; see also Ricoeur 1990 and Geertz 1973.

10. See Gibbal 1988; Leiris [1958] 1980; Rouget 1980; Schaeffner 1965—a quartet of French writers mesmerized by African (East and West) spirit possession.

11. See Mudimbe 1988; Trinh 1988; and Miller 1990 for trenchant critiques of Eurocentrism in the social sciences.

12. See Stoller 1989a, 1995.

13. Stoller 1995, 22; see also Stoller 1992; Kapferer 1992; Csordas 1990; Kramer 1993; and Taussig 1993 for works on the embodied dimensions of spirit possession. Indeed, Taussig links Hauka spirit possession to the dynamic interplay of what he calls the "mimetic faculty."

14. See Ong 1967.

15. Zuckerkandl 1956; Feld and Rouch 1982. See also E. Basso 1985; Seeger [1987] 2014; Stoller 1989b, 1997; Samuels et al. 2010; Porcello et al. 2010. Sound

specialists have a particularly keen sense of spirit possession, perhaps the key sense in the onset of that altered state.

16. See Rouch and Feld 2003; Stoller 1992; Henley 2009; MacDougall 2005, 1998; Ruby 2000.

17. See Howes 2005; Howes and Classen 2013; Classen and Howes 2005.

18. See Bartoshuck and Duffy 1998; Ihde [1975] 2012; Jay and Ramaswamy 2014; Mizroeff 2012.

19. See Behar 2009, 2013; Taussig 1993; M. D. Jackson 2004; Desjarlais 1992, 1997; Vitebsky 2005; Narayan 1989, 2007. These writers tend to use descriptive prose that shows the power of the senses to shape social relations.

20. See Stoller 1989a, 1989b, 1997, 2002, 2008, 2014.

21. See Said 1985.

22. Stoller 1989a, 1.

23. Rouch 1955.

24. Rouch 1955.

25. Kirshenblatt-Gimblett 1999, 3.

26. Boswell 2017, 193.

27. Boswell 2017, 198.

28. Boswell 2017, 198.

29. Boswell 2017, 206.

30. Sutton 2010, 220.

31. See Petrini 2007.

32. Stoller and Olkes 1987.

4. Tasting Harmony in the World

1. See Stoller and Olkes 1986.

2. Korsmeyer 2005, 1.

3. See Brillat-Savarin [1854] 2014; Bartoshuck and Duffy 1998; Rozin and Rozin 1981.

4. Goody 1982; Bourdieu 1984.

5. Peterson 1994; Khare 1994; Carmichael and Sayer 1991.

6. Kant [1781] 1966; Butler 2019; Gronow 2003; and Peynaud 1987, as well as essays on how taste is linked to emotion and memory (Proust 2003; Seremetakis 1994; Sutton 2010; Boswell 2017).

7. Weismantel 1994.

8. Weismantel 1994.

9. Mintz 1986, 214.

10. Sutton 2010, 212.

11. See Seremetakis 1994; Cowan 1991.

12. Kirshenblatt-Gimblett 1999, 3.

13. Sutton 2010, 220.
14. See Petrini 2007.
15. See Rouch 1956.

5. Peripheral Knowledge and the Imponderables of the Between

1. See Rouch 1960b; Stoller and Olkes 1987; Stoller 2008.
2. See Dewey 1929.
3. Thomas 1999, 109.
4. Chittick 1989, ix–x. This work is a classic text on Sufi belief, a must read for those who want to better understand the mystical elements of Sufism.
5. Crapanzano 2003, 57–58; see also Chittick 1989.
6. Crapanzano 2003, 64–65.
7. Stoller 2008, 170.
8. Rorty 1979, 370.
9. See Geertz 1988.
10. See Merleau-Ponty 1964b.
11. V. Turner 1969, 98.
12. E. Turner 2012, 1.
13. E. Turner 2012, 11.
14. Kapferer 2018.
15. See Geertz 1973.
16. See Martínez, Di Puppo, and Frederiksen 2021.
17. Martínez, Di Puppo, and Frederiksen 2021, 187.

6. The World According to Rouch

1. See Stoller 1992.
2. See Henley 2009, Feld and Rouch 2003, and many others.
3. See Finnegan 2014.
4. See Vannini, Waskul, and Gottschalk 2012; Boswell 2017; Stoller 2019.
5. McGranahan 2020, 27.

7. Wisdom from the Edge of the Village

1. See Stoller 1989a.
2. See Stoller 2002.
3. See Vidal 2014.
4. Cited in Vidal 2014.
5. Ferguson 2021.
6. Ferguson 2021.

7. Ferguson 2021.

8. Flavelle and Goodluck 2021.

9. K. Basso 1996, 107. Basso's magnum opus, *Wisdom Sits in Places*, is one of the most visionary ethnographies I have read. It underscores not only the wisdom of indigenous elders but also the importance of applying that wisdom to confront our social cultural and ecological problems. It is a roadmap to future well-being.

10. Quoted in K. Basso 1996, 127.

11. See Rafferty 2018.

12. See Gibbens 2019.

13. See California Department of Forestry and Fire Protection 2021.

14. See Throop 2022.

15. See Mwai 2021.

16. Khan and Patrick 2016, 79; also cited in Lynteris 2019, 66; see also Ialenti 2020.

17. See Leiss 1994.

18. See Bookchin 2005.

19. Morton and Boyer 2021, 62; Ialenti 2020; see also Latour 2021. These texts wonder about the social future of humankind. Latour writes a philosophical fable using Kafka's incomparable text *Metamorphosis* to make sense of how human beings might adapt to the environmental, pandemic, and political circumstances of the contemporary times. How did Gregor Samsa cope with the social and cultural rigidities of his era? How did he "break out" of his unresolvable circumstances? In his concluding chapter he wrote about how "we" have landed on a new pandemically impacted earth. "So you've landed, you've crashed, you've extricated yourself from ground zero, you're advancing, masked, you're voice barely audible: like Gregor's, like mine, it's a sort of mumbling. 'Where am I?' What to do? Go straight ahead as Descartes advised those lost in the forest. No! Fan out. Explore all your capacities for survival, conspire, as hard as you can, with the agencies that have made the places you've landed habitable. Under the canopy of the heavens, now heavy again, other humans mingled with other materials form other peoples with other living things. They are freeing themselves at last. They are coming out of lockdown. They're being metamorphosed" (128). Latour's work was creative and poetic, but I'm not sure his use of Kafka's work sufficiently underscored his message about the viability of *Homo sapiens*. In *Deep Time Reckoning* Ialenti (2020) is more concrete than Latour. He suggests a system of education that promotes long-term as opposed to short-term thinking, a kind of training that encompasses attunement: "a principled embrace of receptivity, sensitivity, and appreciation of one's wider world. To embrace attunement is to resist yearning for mastery, escapism, or mechanistic thinking" (157). This idea corresponds to Morton and Boyer's notion of how we become human again, which, in turn, resonates with the thinking of indigenous elders like Adamu Jenitongo, Davi Kopenawa, and Dudley Patterson.

20. See Jackson 2011 for more on life within limits. Such a tack has enabled Songhay people to live full lives in existentially challenging circumstances.

21. Morton and Boyer 2021, 13–14.

22. Morton and Boyer 2021, 13–14.

Coda

1. See Kolbert 2014; Odell 2019. For Odell doing nothing has nothing to do with slacking; it is about learning how to pay attention—a kind of attunement to one's surroundings. Her theme is like that of Latour, but more direct. "But beyond self-care and the ability to (really) listen, the practice of doing nothing has something broader to offer us: an antidote to the rhetoric of growth. In the context of health and ecology, things that grow unchecked are often considered parasitic or cancerous. Yet we inhabit a culture that privileges novelty and growth over the cyclical and the regenerative. Our very idea of productivity is promised on the idea of producing something new, whereas we do not tend to see maintenance and care in the same way" (25).

2. See Vine et al. 2021.

3. See Vine et al. 2021.

Works Cited

Agee, James, and Walker Evans. 1941. *Let Us Now Praise Famous Men*. New York: Houghton Mifflin.

Arendt, Hanna. 1958. *The Human Condition*. Chicago: University of Chicago Press.

Arntsen, Bjørn, and Lisbet Holtedahl. 2005. "Visualising Situatedness: The Role of the Audience/Reader in Knowledge Production." In *Challenging Situatedness: Gender, Culture, and the Productions of Knowledge*, edited by Erica Englestad and Siri Gerrard, 67–83. Chicago: University of Chicago Press.

Badkhen, Anna. 2015. *Walking with Abel: Journeys with the Nomads of the African Savannah*. New York: Riverhead.

Badkhen, Anna. 2018. *Fisherman's Blues: A West African Community at Sea*. New York: Riverhead.

Balandier, Georges. 1966. *Ambiguous Africa*. London: Chatto & Windus.

Bartoshuck, Linda, and Valerie Duffy. 1998. "Chemical Senses." In *Comparative Psychology: A Handbook*, edited by Gary Greenberg and Maury Haraway, 282–90. New York: Routledge.

Bascombe, William. 1969. *Ifa Divination: Between Gods and Men in West Africa*. Bloomington: Indiana University Press.

Basso, Ellen. 1985. *A Musical View of the Universe: Kalapalo Myth and Ritual Performances*. Philadelphia: University of Pennsylvania Press.

Basso, Keith. 1996. *Wisdom Sits in Places*. Albuquerque: University of New Mexico Press.

Bastide, Roger. 1978. *The African Religions of Brazil*. Baltimore: Johns Hopkins University Press.

BBC 2021. "Covid-19 Africa: What Is Happening with Vaccine Supplies," June 22. https://www.bbc.com/news/56100076.

Behar, Ruth. 1996. *The Vulnerable Observer: Anthropology That Breaks Your Heart*. Boston: Beacon.

Behar, Ruth. 2009. *An Island Called Home*. New Brunswick, NJ: Rutgers University Press.

Behar, Ruth. 2013. *Traveling Heavy*. Durham, NC: Duke University Press.

Berg, Margaret, and Barbara Seeber. 2016. *The Slow Professor: Challenging the Culture of Speed in the Academy*. Toronto: University of Toronto Press.

Bessire, Lucas. 2021. *Running Out: In Search of Water on the High Plains*. Princeton, NJ: Princeton University Press.

Boadle, Anthony. 2021. "Gold Miners Fire on Yanomami Indigenous Community in Brazil." Reuters, May 11. https://www.reuters.com/world/americas/illegal-gold-miners-fire-yanomami-indigenous-community-brazil-2021-05-11/.

Boddy, Janice. 1989. *Wombs and Alien Spirits*. Madison: University of Wisconsin Press.

Bookchin, Murray. [1985] 2005. *The Ecology of Freedom: The Emergence and Dissolution of Hierarchy*. Oakland, CA: AK Press.

Boswell, Rose. 2017. "Sensuous Stories in the Indian Ocean Islands." *Senses and Society* 12(2): 193–208.

Bourdieu, Pierre. 1984. *Distinction*. Translated by Richard Nice. Cambridge, MA: Harvard University Press.

Bourguignon, Erica. 1976. *Possession*. San Francisco: Chandler & Sharp.

Brillat-Savarin, Jean-Anthelme. [1854] 2014. *The Physiology of Taste*. Translated from the last Paris edition by Fayette Robinson. Adelaide: University of Adelaide Press.

Bruner, Jerome. 1991. "The Narrative Construction of Reality." *Critical Inquiry* 18(1): 1–21.

Buber, Martin. 1971. *I and Thou*. Translated by Walter Kaufmann. New York: Scribners.

Butler, Ella. 2019. "Taste Environments." Fieldsites, April 25. https://culanth.org/fieldsites/taste-environments.

California Department of Forestry and Fire Protection. 2021. *Fire Statistics*. Sacramento: State of California.

Carmichael, Elizabeth, and Chloe Sayer. 1991. *The Skeleton at the Feast: The Day of the Dead*. Austin: University of Texas Press.

Chabon, Michael. 1995. *Wonder Boys*. New York: Picador.

Charbonnier, Georges. 1959. *Le monologue du peintre*. Paris: Julliard.

Chernoff, John Miller. 1979. *African Rhythm and African Sensibility*. Chicago: University of Chicago Press.

Chittick, William C. 1989. *The Sufi Path of Knowledge: Ibn al-'Arabi's Meta-physics of the Imagination*. Albany: State University of New York Press.

Classen, Constance, and David Howes. 2005. *The Book of Touch*. Oxford: Berg.

Cowan, Jane. 1991. "Going Out for Coffee? Contesting the Grounds of Gendered Pleasures." In *Contested Identities: Gender and Kinship in Modern Greece*, edited by P. Loizos and E. Papataksiarchis, 180–202. Princeton, NJ: Princeton University Press.

Cox, Rupert, Andrew Irving, and Chris Wright, eds. 2016. *Beyond Text? Critical Practices and Sensory Anthropology*. Manchester: Manchester University Press.

Crapanzano, Vincent. 1980. *Tuhami: Portrait of a Moroccan*. Chicago: University of Chicago Press.

Crapanzano, Vincent. 2003. *Imaginative Horizons: An Essay in Literary-Philosophical Anthropology*. Chicago: University of Chicago Press.

Csordas, Thomas. 1990. "Embodiment as a Paradigm for Anthropology." *Ethos* 18(1): 5–47.

De Boeck, Filip. 2015. "Divining the City: Rhythm, Amalgamation, and Knotting as Forms of 'Urbanity.'" *Social Dynamics* 41(1): 47–58.

De Boeck, Filip, and René Devisch. 1994. "Ndembu, Lunda and Yaka Divination Compared: From Representation and Social Engineering to Embodiment and Worldmaking." *Journal of Religion in Africa* 22(2): 98–128.

Derrida, Jacques. 1984. "Deconstruction of the Other: Interview with Richard Kearney." In *Dialogues with Contemporary Continental Thinkers: The Phenomenology of Heritage*, edited by Richard Kearney, 107–26. Manchester: Manchester University Press.

Desjarlais, Robert. 1992. *Body and Emotion*. Philadelphia: University of Pennsylvania Press.

Desjarlais, Robert. 1997. *Shelter Blues: Sanity and Selfhood among the Homeless*. Philadelphia: University of Pennsylvania Press.

Devisch, Renaat. 1985. "Perspectives on Divination in Contemporary Sub-Saharan Africa." In *Theoretical Explorations in African Religion*, edited by Wim Binsbergen and Matthew Schoffeleers, 50–84. London: KPI Paul International.

Devisch, Renaat. 1991. "Mediumistic Divination among the Northern Yaka of Zaire." In *African Divination Systems*, edited by Phillip Peek, 112–33. Bloomington: Indiana University Press.

Dewey, John. 1929. *The Quest for Certainty*. New York: Minton, Balch.

Downey, Greg. 2005. *Learning Capoeira: Lessons in Cunning from Afro-Brazilian Art*. New York: Oxford University Press.

Durkheim, Emile. 1912. *The Elementary Forms of Religious Life*. Translated by Joseph Swain. London: Allen & Unwin.

Eco, Umberto. 1979. *A Theory of Semiotics*. Bloomington: Indiana University Press.

Eliot, T. S. 1968. *The Four Quartets*. New York: Mariner.

Englested, Erica, and Siri Gerrard, eds. 2005. *Challenging Situatedness: Gender, Culture, and the Production of Knowledge*. Chicago: University of Chicago Press.

Faye, Gaël. 2018. *Small Country: A Novel*. Translated by Sarah Ardizzone. London: Hogarth.

Feld, Stephen, and Jean Rouch. 2003. *Cine-Ethnography*. Minneapolis: University of Minnesota Press.

Ferguson, Bernard. 2021. "Climate Change Is Destroying My Country." *New York Times*, June 23. https://www.nytimes.com/2021/06/23/magazine/climate-change-impact-bahamas.html.

Finnegan, Ruth. 2014. *Communicating: Multi-Modes of Human Interconnection*: London: Routledge.

Flavelle, Christopher, and Kalen Goodluck. 2021. "Dispossessed Again: Climate Change Hits Native Americans Especially Hard." *New York Times*, June 27. https://www.nytimes.com/2021/06/27/climate/climate-Native-Americans.html.

Frasier, James. 1890. *The Golden Bough*. New York: Macmillan.

Friedson, Steven. 1996. *Dancing Prophets: Musical Experience in Tumbuka Healing*. Chicago: University of Chicago Press.

Gardner, Robert. 1980. *Screening Room: Jean Rouch*. 64 min. Watertown, MA. Documentary Educational Resources.

Geertz, Clifford. 1973. *The Interpretation of Cultures*. New York: Basic Books.

Geertz, Clifford. 1988. *Works and Lives: The Anthropologist as Author*. New York: Polity.

Gell, Alfred. 1980. "The Gods at Play: Vertigo and Possession in Muria Religion." *Man* (n.s.) 15: 219–49.

Ghodsee, Kirsten. 2016. *From Notes to Narrative: Writing Ethnographies That Everyone Can Read*. Chicago: University of Chicago Press.

Gibbal, Jean-Marie. 1988. *Les génies du fleuve*. Paris: Presses de la Renaissance.

Gibbens, Sarah. 2019. "Hurricane Sandy, Explained." *National Geographic*, February 11. https://www.nationalgeographic.com/environment/article/hurricane-sandy.

Goodman, Felicitas. 1990. *Where Spirits Ride the Wind: Trance Journeys and Other Ecstatic Experiences*. Bloomington: Indiana University Press.

Goody, Jack. 1982. *Cooking, Cuisine and Class*. Cambridge: Cambridge University Press.

Gottschall, Jonathan. 2012. *The Storytelling Animal*. New York: Houghton Mifflin.

Griaule, Marcel, and Germaine Dieterlen. 1969. *Le renard pâle*. Paris: Institut de l'ethnologie.

Gronow, Jukka. 2003. *Caviar with Champagne: Common Luxury and the Ideals of the Good Life in Stalin's Russia*. Oxford: Berg.

Hamdy, Sherine, and Coleman Nye. 2017. *Lissa: A Story of Medical Promise, Friendship and Revolution*. Toronto: University of Toronto Press.

Hammer, Joshua. 2016. *The Bad-Ass Librarians of Timbuktu*. New York: Simon & Schuster.

Harris, Grace. 1957. "Possession Hysteria in a Kenya Tribe." *American Anthropologist* 59(6): 1046–66.

Henley, Paul. 2009. *The Adventure of the Real: Jean Rouch and the Craft of Ethnographic Cinema*. Chicago: University of Chicago Press.

Holbrand, Martin. 2012. *Thunder in Motion: The Recursive Anthropology of Cuban Divination*. Chicago: University of Chicago Press.

Holtedahl, Lisbet. 1995. *The Sultan's Burden*. New York: Filmmakers Library.

Holtedahl, Lisbet. 2018. *Wives*. Tromsø: UIT.

Howes, David. 2005. *Empire of the Senses*. 2004. Oxford: Berg.

Howes, David. 2022. *The Sensory Studies Manifesto: Tracking the Sensory Revolution in the Arts and the Human Sciences*. Toronto: University of Toronto Press.

Howes, David, and Constance Classen. 2013. *Ways of Sensing: Understanding the Senses in Society*. New York: Routledge.

Hurston, Zora Neale. 1935. *Mules and Men*. Philadelphia: J. D. Lippincott.

Ialenti, Vincent. 2020. *Deep Time Reckoning: How Future Thinking Can Help Earth Now*. Cambridge, MA: MIT Press.

Ihde, Don. [1975] 2012. *Listening and Voice: The Phenomenology of Sound*. 2nd ed. Albany: SUNY Press.

Jackson, Alfred. 1968. "Sound and Ritual." *Man* (n.s.) 3: 293–300.

Jackson, Michael D. 2004. *In Sierra Leone*. Durham, NC: Duke University Press.

Jackson, Michael D. 2011. *Life within Limits: Well-being in a World of Want*. Durham, NC: Duke University Press.

Jackson, Michael D. 2016a. *As Wide as the World Is Wise: Reinventing Philosophical Anthropology*. New York: Columbia University Press.

Jackson, Michael D. 2016b. *The Work of Art: Rethinking the Elementary Forms of Religious Life*. New York: Columbia University Press.

Jain, S. Locklann. 2019. *Things That Art: A Graphic Menagerie of Enchanting Curiosity*. Toronto: University of Toronto Press.

Jay, Martin, and Sumanthi Ramaswamy. 2014. *Empires of Vision*. Durham, NC: Duke University Press.

Kant, Immanuel. [1781] 1966. *The Critique of Judgment*. New York: Hafner.

Kapferer, Bruce. 1992. Review of *Fusion of the Worlds*. *American Ethnologist* 19(3): 846–47.

Kapferer, Bruce. 2018. Interview. *University of Bergen Magazine*, October 19.

Kehoe, Alice, and Dodi Giletti. 1981. "Women's Preponderance in Possession Cults: The Calcium-Deficiency Hypothesis Extended." *American Anthropologist* 83: 549–62.

Khan, Ali S., and William Patrick. 2016. *The Next Pandemic: On the Front Lines against Humankind's Gravest Dangers*. New York: Public Affairs.

Khare, R. S., ed. 1994. *The Eternal Food: Gastronomic Ideas and Experiences of Hindus and Buddhists*. Albany: SUNY University Press.

Kirshenblatt-Gimblett, Barbara 1999. "Playing to the Senses: Food as Performance Medium. *On Cooking* 4(1): 1–30.

Kolbert, Elizabeth. 2014. *The Sixth Extinction: An Unnatural History*. New York: Picador.

Korsmeyer, Carolyn, ed. 2005. *The Taste Culture Reader*. Oxford: Berg.

Kramer, Fritz. 1993. *The Red Fez: Art and Spirit Possession in Africa*. London: Verso.

Lambek, Michael. 1981. *Human Spirits*. London: Cambridge University Press.

Landry, Timothy. 2019. *Vodun: Secrecy and the Search for Divine Power*. Philadelphia: University of Pennsylvania Press.

Latour, Bruno. 2021. *After Lockdown: A Metamorphosis*. Cambridge: Polity.

Leiris, Michel. [1958] 1980. *La possession et ses aspects théâtraux chez les Ethiopiens de Gondar*. Paris: Le Sycamore.

Leiss, William. 1972. *The Domination of Nature*. Montreal: McGill–Queen's University Press.

Lewis, Ion. 1971. *Ecstatic Religion: An Anthropological Study of Spirit Possession and Shamanism*. London: Penguin.

Lynteris, Chistos. 2019. *Human Extinction and the Pandermic Imaginary*. London: Routledge.

MacDougall, David. 1998. *Transcultural Cinema*. Princeton, NJ: Princeton University Press.

MacDougall, David. 2005. *The Corporal Body: Film, Ethnography, and the Senses*. Princeton, NJ: Princeton University Press.

Martínez, Francisco, Lili Di Puppo, and Martin Demant Frederiksen, eds. 2021. *Peripheral Methodologies: Unlearning, Not-knowing, and Ethnographic Limits*. London: Routledge.

Martinez, Wilton. 1992. "Who Constructs Anthropological Knowledge? Toward a Theory of Film Spectatorship." In *Film as Ethnography*, edited by D. Turton and P. Crawford, 130–61. Manchester: Manchester University Press.

McGranahan, Carole. 2020. "Anthropology as Theoretical Storytelling." In *Writing Anthropology: Essays on Craft and Commitment*, edited by Carole McGranahan, 23–27. Durham, NC: Duke University Press.

Merleau-Ponty, Maurice. 1964. *L'oeil et l'esprit*. Paris: Gallimard.

Merleau-Ponty, Maurice. 1969. *La prose du monde*. Paris: Gallimard.

Miller, Christopher. 1990. *Theories of Africans*. Chicago: University of Chicago Press.

Mintz, Sidney. 1986. *Sweetness and Power*. New York: Penguin.

Mizroeff, Nicholas. 2012. *Visual Culture Reader*. 3rd ed. New York: Routledge.

Monfouga-Nicholas, Jacqueline. 1972. *Ambivalence et culte de possession*. Paris: Editions Anthropos.

Morton, Timothy, and Dominic Boyer. 2021. *Hyposubjects: On Becoming Human*. London: Open Humanities Press.

Mosley, Walter. 2005. *Cinnamon Kiss*. New York: Little, Brown.

Mudimbe, Valentin. 1988. *The Invention of Africa*. Bloomington: Indiana University Press.

Mwai, Peter. 2021. "Covid-19 Vaccinations: African Nations Miss WHO Target." *BBC News*, December 31. https://www.bbc.com/news/56100076.

Narayan, Kirin. 1989. *Storytellers, Saints and Scoundrels*. Philadelphia: University of Pennsylvania Press.

Narayan, Kirin. 2007. *My Family and Other Saints*. Chicago: University of Chicago Press.

Narayan, Kirin. 2012. *Alive in the Writing: Crafting Ethnography in the Company of Chekhov*. Chicago: University of Chicago Press.

Nietzsche, Friedrich. [1876] 1956. *The Birth of Tragedy Out of the Spirit of Music*. Translated by Francis Goffling. Garden City, NJ: Doubleday / Anchor.

Obeysekere, Gananath. 1981. *Medusa's Hair: An Essay on Personal Symbols and Religious Experience*. Chicago: University of Chicago Press.

Odell, Jenny. 2019. *How to Do Nothing: Resisting the Attention Economy*. New York: Melville House.

Ong, Walter. 1967. *The Presence of the Word*. New Haven, CT: Yale University Press.

Peek, Philip, ed. 1991. *African Divination Systems: Ways of Knowing*. Bloomington: Indiana University Press.

Peterson, Sarah. 1994. *Acquired Taste: The French Origins of Modern Cooking.* Ithaca, NY: Cornell University Press.

Petrini, Carlo. 2007. *Slow Food Nation: Why Our Food Should Be Good, Clean and Fair.* New York: Rizzoli.

Peynaud, Emile. 1987. *The Taste of Wine.* New York: Wiley.

Pidoux, Charles. 1955. "Les états de possession chez les melanos-africains." *Evolution psychiatrique* 2.

Porcello, Thomas, Louise Meintjes, Ana Maria Ochoa, and David W. Samuels. 2010. "The Reorganization of the Sensory World." *Annual Review of Anthropology* 39: 51–66.

Pratt, Mary Louise. 1986. "Conventions of Representation: Where Discourse and Ideology Meet." In *Georgetown University Roundtable in Languages and Linguistics*, edited by Heidi Bynes, 139–55. Washington, DC: Georgetown University Press.

Predal, René. 1982. *Jean Rouch: un griot gaullois.* Paris: Harmattan.

Proust, Marcel. 2003. *Swann's Way.* Vol. 1 of *Remembrance of Things Past.* Adelaide: University of Adelaide Press.

Rafferty, John P. 2018. "Hurricane Katrina." *Britannica.com.* https://www.britannica.com/event/Hurricane-Katrina.

Ricoeur, Paul. 1990. *Oneself as Another.* Translated by Kathleen Blamey. Chicago: University of Chicago Press.

Riesman, Paul. 1977. *Freedom in Fulani Social Life.* Chicago: University of Chicago Press.

Rorty, Richard. 1979. *Philosophy and the Mirror of Nature.* Princeton, NJ: Princeton University Press.

Rouch, Jean. 1952. *Bataille sur le grande fleuve.* Paris: IFAN / CNC / Musée de l'Homme.

Rouch, Jean. 1955. *Les maîtres fous.* Paris: Films de la Pléiade.

Rouch, Jean. 1958. *Moi, un noir.* Paris: Films de la Pléiade.

Rouch, Jean. 1959. *La pyramide humaine.* Paris: Films de la Pléiade.

Rouch, Jean. 1960a. *Chronique d'un été.* Paris: Films de la Pléiade.

Rouch, Jean. 1960b. *La religion et la magie Songhay.* Paris: Presses Universitaires de France.

Rouch, Jean. 1970. *Jaguar.* Paris: Films de la Pléiade.

Rouch, Jean. 1972. *Les tambours d'avant: Tourou et Bitti.* Paris: CNRS.

Rouch, Jean, and Steven Feld. 2003. *Cine-Ethnography.* Minneapolis: University of Minnesota Press.

Rouget, Gilbert. 1980. *La musique et la transe.* Paris: Gallimard.

Rozin, Elizabeth, and Paul Rozin. 1981. "Culinary Themes and Variations." *Natural History*, February: 6–14.

Ruby, Jay. 2000. *Picturing Culture: Explorations of Film and Anthropology.* Chicago: University of Chicago Press.

Said, Edward. 1985. *Beginnings: Intention and Method.* New York: Columbia University Press.

Samuels, David, Louise Meintjes, Ana Maria Ochoa, and Thomas Porcello. 2010. "Soundscapes: Toward a Sounded Anthropology." *Annual Review of Anthropology* 39(1): 329–45.

Schaeffner, André. 1965. "Rituel et pre-théâtre." In *Histoire des spectacles,* 21–54. Paris: Gallimard.

Schneider, Arnd. 2016. "Appropriations across Disciplines: The Future of Art and Anthropology Collaborations." In *Beyond Text? Critical Practices and Sensory Anthropology,* edited by Rupert Cox, Andrew Irving, and Chris Wright, 20–33. Manchester: Manchester University Press.

Seeger, Anthony. [1987] 2014. *Why Suya Sing: A Musical Anthropology of an Amazonian People.* Urbana: University of Illinois Press.

Seremetakis, C. Nadia, ed. 1994. *The Senses Still.* Boulder, CO: Westview.

Shack, William, and Elliot P. Skinner. 1979. *Strangers in African Societies.* Berkeley: University of California Press.

Shaw, Rosalind. 1991. "Splitting Truths from Darkness: Epistemological Aspects of Temne Divination." In *African Divination Systems,* edited by Philip M. Peek, 137–52. Bloomington: Indiana University Press.

Stoller, Paul. 1989a. *Fusion of the Worlds: An Ethnography of Possession among the Songhay of Niger.* Chicago: University of Chicago Press.

Stoller, Paul. 1989b. *The Taste of Ethnographic Things.* Philadelphia: University of Pennsylvania Press.

Stoller, Paul. 1992. *The Cinematic Griot: The Ethnography of Jean Rouch.* Chicago: University of Chicago Press.

Stoller, Paul. 1995. *Embodying Colonial Memories.* New York: Routledge.

Stoller, Paul. 1997. *Sensuous Scholarship.* Philadelphia: University of Pennsylvania Press.

Stoller, Paul. 2002. *Money Has No Smell: The Africanization of New York City.* Chicago: University of Chicago Press.

Stoller, Paul. 2004. *Stranger in the Village of the Sick.* Boston: Beacon.

Stoller, Paul. 2008. *The Power of the Between: An Anthropological Odyssey.* Chicago: University of Chicago Press.

Stoller, Paul. 2013. "Religion and the Truth of Being." In *A Companion to the Anthropology of Religion,* edited by Janice Boddy and Michael Lambek, 154–69. Oxford: Wiley Blackwell.

Stoller, Paul. 2014. *Yaya's Story: The Quest for Well-Being in the World.* Chicago: University of Chicago Press.

Stoller, Paul. 2017. "Sorcery and the Supernatural in Niger and Mali." In *Religion: Super Religion*, edited by Jeffrey Kripal, 219–30. New York: Macmillan.

Stoller, Paul. 2018. *Adventures in Blogging: Public Anthropology and Popular Media*. Toronto: University of Toronto Press.

Stoller, Paul. 2020a. "Conclusion: The World According to Rouch." In *The Routledge Handbook of Ethnographic Film and Video*, edited by Phillip Vannini, 348–54. New York: Routledge.

Stoller, Paul. 2020b. "Ghana on My Mind." *Psychology Today*, February 25.

Stoller, Paul. 2020c. "Imaging Knowledge: Anthropology, Storytelling and the Quest for Well-Being in a Troubled World." *Swedish Journal of Anthropology* 3(1–2): 11–21.

Stoller, Paul, and Cheryl Olkes. 1986. "Bad Sauce, Good Ethnography." *Cultural Anthropology* 1: 336–52.

Stoller, Paul, and Cheryl Olkes. 1987. *In Sorcery's Shadow: A Memoir of Apprenticeship among the Songhay of Niger*. Chicago: University of Chicago Press.

Sturtevant, William. 1968. "Categories, Percussion and Physiology." *Man* (n.s.) 3: 133–34.

Sutton, David. 2010. "Food and the Senses." *Annual Review of Anthropology* 39: 209–23.

Taussig, Michael. 1993. *Mimesis and Alterity*. New York: Routledge.

Taylor, Mark. 2014. "Speed Kills: Fast Is Never Fast Enough." *Chronicle of Higher Education*, October 20.

Thomas, Nigel J. T. 1999. "Are Theories of Images Theories of the Imagination?" *Cognitive Science* 23: 207–45.

Throop, Jason. 2022. "Looming." *Puncta: Journal of Critical Phenomenology* 5(3): 67–86.

Trinh, T. Min-ha. 1988. *Woman, Native, Other*. Bloomington: Indiana University Press.

Trundle, Catherine. 2014. *Americans in Tuscany: Charity, Compassion and Belonging*. New York: Berghahn.

Turkle, Sherry. 2016. *Reclaiming Conversation: The Power of Talk in the Digital Age*. New York: Penguin.

Turner, Edith. 2012. *Communitas: The Anthropology of Collective Joy*. New York: Palgrave.

Turner, Victor. 1969. *The Ritual Process: Structure and Anti-Structure*. Ithaca, NY: Cornell University Press.

Tylor, Edward. 1871. *Primitive Culture*. London: Cambridge University Press.

Ulysse, Gina Athena. 2017. *Because When God Is Too Busy: Haiti, Me & the World*. Middletown, CT: Wesleyan University Press.

Vannini, Phillip, Dennis Waskul, and Simon Gottschalk, eds. 2012. *The Sensed in Self, Society, and Culture: The Sociology of the Senses*. London: Routledge.

Vidal, John. 2014. "People in the West Live Squeezed Together, Frenzied as Wasps in the Nest." *Guardian*, December 30.

Vine, David, David Gellner, Mark Schuller, Alpha Shah, and Gwen Middleton. 2021. "Collaborative Manifesto for Political Anthropology in an Age of Crises." *Anthropology News*, July 16. https://www.anthropology-news. org/articles/collaborative-manifesto-for-political-anthropology-in-an-age-of-crises/.

Vitebsky, Piers. 2005. *The Reindeer People*. New York: Houghton Mifflin Harcourt.

Wacquant, Loic. 2004. *Body and Soul: Ethnographic Notebooks of an Apprentice Boxer*. New York: Oxford University Press.

Waterston, Alisse. 2013. *My Father's Wars*. New York: Routledge.

Waterston, Alisse, and Charlotte Corden. 2020. *Light in Dark Times: The Human Search for Meaning*. Toronto: University of Toronto Press.

Weismantel, Mary. 1994. "Tasty Meals and Bitter Gifts." *Food and Foodways* 5(1): 79–94.

Werbner, Richard. 2015. *Divination's Grasp: African Encounters with the Almost Said*. Bloomington: Indiana University Press.

Whitehouse, Bruce. 2012. *Migrants and Strangers in an African City*. Bloomington: Indiana University Press.

Wittgenstein, Ludwig. 1953. *Philosophical Investigations*. Translated by G. E. M. Anscombe. New York: Macmillan.

Wulff, Helena, ed. 2016. *The Anthropologist as Writer: Genres and Contexts in the 21st Century*. London: Berghahn.

Zempleni, Andras. 1968. *L'interprétation et la thérapie traditionnelles du désordre mental chez les Wolof et les Lebou (Sénégal)*. Paris: Institut d'Ethnologie.

Zuckerkandl, Victor. 1956. *Sound and Symbol: Music and the External World*. Translated by Willard R. Trask. Princeton, NJ: Princeton University Press.

Index

Page numbers in *italics* refer to figures.

www.ingramcontent.com/pod-product-compliance
Lightning Source LLC
Chambersburg PA
CBHW020533270326
41927CB00006B/559